Students of Thought

Personal Journeys

Students of Thought
Personal Journeys

R. Wayne Shute
Sharon Gibb

Detselig Enterprises Ltd.

Calgary, Alberta

© 1993
R. Wayne Shute
Brigham Young University, Provo, Utah

Sharon Gibb
Mount Royal College, Calgary, Alberta

Canadian Cataloguing in Publication Data

Shute, R. Wayne,
    Students of thought : personal journeys

    Includes bibliographical references.
    ISBN 1-55059-070-7
    1. Education – Philosophy.   2. Teaching.
3. Teachers – Attitudes.   4. Thought and
thinking.   I. Gibb, Sharon, 1943-   II. Title.
LB1025.3.S58 1993   370'.1   C93-091320-5

Detselig Enterprises Ltd.
210, 1220 Kensington Road N.W.
Calgary, Alberta T2N 3P5

This book is available in the U.S. from Temeron Books, Inc., P.O. Box 896,
Bellingham, Washington, 98227.

Printed in Canada   SAN 115-0324   ISBN 1-55059-070-7

To all who have helped us
on our journey

Contents

Introduction, Students of Thought. *R. Wayne Shute* . . . 1

1 A Changing Perspective. *Neil Nordquist* 7

2 Thoughtfulness Makes Me Tense. *Toni Kennedy* . . . 21

3 A Journey to Thoughtfulness. *Peter Darby* 33

4 Learning, Teaching, and Leading - Some Observations

   Along the Way. *Garry McKinnon* 43

5 Teacher Stories: Thoughtful Voices from the Classroom.

   Jean Hoeft 61

6 Toward the Forgotten Thoughtfulness. *Irene Naested* . 75

7 I'm Thinking of Leaving Teaching. *Sharon Gibb* . . . 89

8 A Web of Understanding. *Judy Hehr* 99

9 Wasted Times, Wasted Thoughts. *Altha Neilson* . . . 111

10 Thinking About Truth. *Ron Patrick* 123

   References 135

Introduction
Students of Thought

R. Wayne Shute

The Journey Metaphor

The journey metaphor is often used to describe our mortal "intellectual or spiritual"[1] sojourn. The probable root of this journey metaphor comes from the classical Greek mythological hero journey. Here we find a hero who faces overwhelming obstacles, finds himself in strange and frightening far-away places, and must contend, even with the gods at times, before he is reunited with loved ones and returns to the safety of his home.

Homer's *The Odyssey* is the most famous of the classical stories. King Odysseus represents the model of a man of courage and determination – in spite of many setbacks, he never abandons his goal of returning home.

> And when long years and seasons wheeling brought around that point of time
> ordained for him to make his passage homeward, trials and dangers, even so,
> attended him even in Ithaka, near those he loved.
>
> Yet all the gods had pitied Lord Odysseus, all but Poseidon, raging cold and
> rough against the brave king till he came ashore at last on his own land.[2]

The hero journey is a popular metaphor and is woven into "more elaborate epics of Gaels, Aztecs, Hindoos, Tarters, South Sea Islanders, Finns, Russians, Scandinavians, and Eskimo."[3]

Much can be made of the hero journey metaphor. We can make it competitive – we can view life's journey as a series of adversarial adventures. We can view the environment, for example, as hostile, something to be conquered and subdued. We can also see our fellow humans as enemies and see life as a battle, where we "beat the other guy" and, thereby, succeed ourselves. This adversarial mindset derives, no doubt, from the ancient Procrustean cycle. When a stranger entered a country he was required to behave according to accepted norms of behavior. In each case he was "measured" on a Procrustean altar or bed to see if he "fit" the norm. If he didn't, he was cast out of the land or, more commonly, "made to fit" or put to death.

Or, we can take an opposite view, a more kind and gentle one. We can see life as Eastern mystics or Biblical prophets saw it – an opportunity to live in harmony with people and nature; life as an opportunity to do good to others and the environment around us.

1

We can also see the journey metaphor in the context of discovering self, of trying to come to grips with who we are, why we are here in mortality and where we are going. We can see it as a journey of self discovery, an internal one, where we seek unceasingly for the meaning of life and all its activities.

T.S. Eliot saw the journey as an exploration to discover our beginnings.

We shall not cease from exploration
And the end of all our exploring
Will be to arrive where we started
And know the place for the first time.[4]

And powerful indeed are the lines,

What we call the beginning is often the end
And to make an end is to make a beginning.[5]

On a Journey to Thoughtful Teaching and Learning

The ten educators whose intriguing stories appear in this book, have rightly chosen the hero journey metaphor to describe their on-going search for meaning regarding teaching and learning. And in so doing, they have discovered themselves in a broad context – well beyond their professional work.

Their journeys have been heroic in the sense that they have oftentimes been difficult and, at times, disappointing. They were willing, however, to press on and explore an ever-widening mind puzzle of themselves.

They began their doctoral degree programs at Brigham Young University in the Summer of 1990 and were introduced to what seemed for some of them a rather radical view of teaching and learning. They were invited, in spite of some disagreements, to take a journey to try to understand what we have come to call "thoughtful teaching and learning."

I suspect the journey would have been impossible had it not been for the cohort nature of the study program. They worked, for the most part cooperatively, and at other times they pushed each other to strained argument and tense debate. There was also an episode or enormous suffering which "broke the heart" but rallied all of us to a more important consideration of the meaning of life.

Out of these experiences has emerged a group of life-long colleagues willing, I believe, to sacrifice for each other in ways uncommon, even among friends.

Thoughtful Teaching and Learning

What is this "thoughtful teaching and learning" that has given focus to the journey of our ten educators? To begin with, I will give a brief description of what thoughtful teaching and learning is not. The usual conception of learning is that students "acquire" through listening, reading, and completing various assignments, a number of concepts, principles or facts about a given subject. Students are usually required to demonstrate their acquisition of the facts through tests or some form of evaluation to assure that they have grasped them. This kind of teaching and learning is perhaps best described by the "transmission metaphor" where teachers see learners as mere robots into which information is tediously transmitted.

Now a few thoughts about what I conceive thoughtful teaching and learning to be. I note a few fundamental principles which describe thoughtful teaching and learning as follows:

The first fundamental principle is that perspective (sometimes called zeitgeist, world perspective, or world view) essentially governs and determines all of our behaviors and actions. This means that we are "products" – some people would say "victims" - of the power of the perspective that makes up the fabric, the warp and woof, of our society. Perspective is such a powerful force in our lives that, in fact, we are not much of a match when up against it.

If our world perspective goes unexamined, two problems will become painfully evident. The first is that we reflect, unwittingly, the perspective which governs the society in which we live. This means, as Rifkin has said, a world view or perspective is successful inasmuch that it goes unquestioned in our lives.[6] For example, even though we may want to reform the present school system, we aren't able to simply because we take for granted the perspective upon which the school system is based. We can massage the system, even go through a mot of motion as if we are bringing fundamental reform to it, but in reality, as Gibboney has clearly shown, not much happens by way of substantive change.[7] The current perspective on education, to take another example, considers learners as technological beings instead of humans who have the power to construct meaning. and try as we may to be something other than automatons, we have great difficulty, unless there is a change in fundamental perspective which is, in our case, technological and, I should add, extremely potent and powerful.

Secondly, if unexamined, the prevailing perspective obviously cannot be changed. Perspective is something that doesn't change easily, but there is at least some hope of changing it if we are aware of what it is and have some idea of its power. But if we are unaware of the driving forces of our prevailing perspective, there is no hope to change it – from our present technological perspective to a human one.

The second fundamental principle of thoughtful teaching and learning is derived from the ancient "initiation metaphor" where the learner is invited as a full fledged member into a "club" of literate people.[8] In this club, people are not only interested in the acquisition of information but they are always concerned with elaborating or operating on that information in order to make *personal meaning* of it or, said another way, to understand its meaning.

The third fundamental principle of thoughtful teaching and learning is that language is of far greater important than is normally allowed. Most teachers are skeptical of this claim because they view language solely as a subject-matter rather than an instrument or tool for *making meaning.*

The fourth principle is that humans may choose to be either thoughtful or thoughtless. The idea of thoughtfulness is not identical to what people normally conceive as natural intelligence. Thoughtfulness is a matter of how we view or approach situations, that is, we are responsible, by choice, for situations in which we find ourselves whether they be thoughtful or thoughtless. Flexibly handling data, resisting rigid categorization of events, being open to new information, adopting multiple perspectives simultaneously – all are character-istics of personal choice in terms of thoughtful interaction with people and the environment. Or, we can choose their opposites which define thoughtlessness, the state, according to Langer, of having the "lights on" when "nobody's home."[9]

The fifth principle is that perplexity is essential to inquiry and, therefore, to the making of meaning - the very heart of learning. From this pedagogical idea come two of the most essential ingredients of learning: perplexity and inquiry.

a. **Perplexity**. Questions are essential to learning but questions cannot be framed until some kind of perplexity or bewilderment is felt by the potential inquirer. If a student's perplexity if not about phenomena treated in the curriculum, but about how to memorize and repeat phrases and words for a quiz or examination, why would we expect those students to raise thoughtful questions about subject matter?

b. **Inquiry**. Public school classrooms are too often places where the rewards for student answers ridiculously outweigh the rewards for student questions. Tragically, provincial curriculum writers and other centralized school leaders presume to already know the questions that students "should ask" and curricula are built around those questions.

The problem is that questions, not answers, are essential to personal meaning, and the questions that begin the search for meaning must be from the learner's mind, not the teacher's. Exclusive dependence on teacher questions can lead, quickly, to thoughtless teaching and little or no learning at all.

The sixth principle is that thoughtful teaching and learning implies not just mindful contemplation of subject matter, but also personal considerateness of other people in the educational setting.

Our Ten Students of Thought

With these few fundamental principles of thoughtful teaching and learning guiding the ten educators, we have in this book, their journeys to becoming "thoughtful." You will find personal sketches of them in the pages of this book – sketches of fascinating people trying to make sense out of the world of teaching and learning.

You'll meet *Neil Nordquist* who explores the idea of world perspective and its impact on education today. He will introduce you to the idea of "predicative teaching and learning" and will suggest that schools should be about the business of fostering personal meaning.

You'll like *Toni Kennedy* who was lulled into "academic euphoria" (while on her journey to thoughtfulness) when she learned how a skier, who has been trapped in an avalanche, need only to *spit* to sense which way is up in order to escape the doom of a white tomb.

Peter Darby started his journey in Nottingham, England and has reached a high level of "awareness" of thoughtfulness through an exploration of the world perspective and its meaning for schools not only for the present but also for the future.

Garry McKinnon spent a great deal of his time, while walking his dog Gizmo, reflecting ("out loud") on the interrelationships between learning, teaching and leading. He's convinced that both he and Gizmo have profited greatly from their "conversations."

Jean Hoeft reached out to other friends and colleagues to help her on her journey. She claims that good teachers have always taught thoughtfully and presents interesting vignettes to validate this claim.

The linking of art and thoughtfulness has been the quest of *Irene Naested*. Her story begins with a "playful" poem and culminates in a wonderful "slice of Greek life" both of which demonstrate her commitment to the arts education.

Sharon Gibb's story of her friend Rhonda who was "thinking of leaving teaching" is in reality her own reflections about the joys (and sorrows) of teaching. Her commitment to helping young people is compelling and breathes "heart" into the work of schools.

Judy Hehr's recent journey is a poignant one. She reminds us that life is fragile and tenuous at best. She helps us see that life (especially the life of a teacher) is about learning which, if understood, breathes new enthusiasm and inspiration into our work.

Most of us will relate to *Altha Neilson*'s journey. She takes us back to our childhood and many painful recollections of school – it could have been otherwise. She helps us see that it could have been a "good place to learn" for both students and teachers.

Ron Patrick's journey seems to be going in the wrong direction. He starts out by knowing "everything" and ends up with only perplexity and questions. He argues, however, that if truth is our guest we must first develop an "interrogative mind."

Your own journey to personal meaning and understanding will be made more meaningful when you read the journeys of these impressive "students of thought."

Notes

[1]*The reader's digest illustrated encyclopedic dictionary,* (Lexical databases, Copyright 1987 by Houghton Mifflin Company). Pleasantville, NY: The Reader's Digest Association, Inc. p. 1180.

[2]Homer. *The Odyssey. (In contemporary verse by Robert Fitzgerald, 1961). Franklin Center, PA: The Franklin Library, p. 4.*

[3]Butcher, S.H., & Lang, A. (no date given). *The Odyssey of Homer.* New York: The Modern Library, pp. xxiii-xxiv.

[4]Eliot, T.S. (1971 – The Centenary Edition). *Four quartets*, New York: A Harvest/HBJ Book. p. 59.

[5]Eliot, Ibid, p. 58.

[6]Rifkin, J. (1980). *Entropy: A new world view.* New York: Viking Press. p. 5.

[7]Gibboney, R. "The killing field of reform." *Phi Delta Kappan*, May 1991. p. 682.

[8]Smith, F. (1988). *Joining the literacy club.* Portsmouth: Heinemann Educational Books, Inc.

[9]Langer, E.J. (1989). *Mindfulness.* Reading, MA: Addison-Wesley Publishing Company, Inc. p. 9.

Neil Nordquist was born in Moose Jaw, Saskatchewan, and was raised in southern Alberta. Neil entered the University of Lethbridge and was one of their first teacher graduates. After teaching in the public schools for three and one-half years, Neil served a two-year mission in the Philippines. He subsequently taught school in Calgary while completing an M.Ed. degree in Educational Administration at the University of Calgary. He has been the principal at several small schools in Alberta, and is currently the principal of a school of seven hundred and fifty students from levels K through twelve in Magrath, Alberta. Neil and his wife, Renee, have seven children ranging in age from two to thirteen years.

1

A Changing Perspective

Neil Nordquist

Meaningful changes within the educational apparatus are not possible unless the entire apparatus itself and its controlling paradigm are placed in a critical . . . perspective. It is our customary and unexamined way of thinking about education, our subliminal assumptions, that must be put in question if significant modifications of practice are to ensue. There is clearly a battle to be fought, but the battlefield is not in the schools as such. It is in our minds, in the attitudes and preconceptions we bring to bear upon education in general, and in our unwitting allegiance to the technological dictates of the era we live in. (p. ix)

David Solway 1989

Solway's statement supports the idea that "perspective drives everything." The way we look at our world determines all we do, all we say, even how we think. Perspective also directs a teacher in his work. We all see what we are prepared to see or what we want to see. All human beings have a basic need to make sense of this world, to feel in control, and to create meaning (Kegan, 1982). The creation of personal meaning forms the perspective by which we then interpret everything in our world. The experiences we have in life form this perspective or frame of reference. Since becoming aware, at a conscious level, of the significance of this concept, I have spent more time considering the experiences and the environment that influence my perspective or frame of reference. I have also become aware of the prevailing perspective of our society, and how that perspective affects me and how it affects education in general. As educators, it is imperative that we consider what affects our view of the world, especially in terms of the impact on learning and teaching.

My family, my faith, my work, the places I have lived, and the experiences I have had all shape the way I view the world. Each of us is the product of

9

similar influences; some experiences are very traumatic, and some are very common. How we were raised, the number of people in our family, the communities we live in, the influence of our extended families, our teachers, and our spiritual experiences are just a few of the things which make us unique. While we are all unique, we do have many similar ideas about how we should behave, and these too come from our experiences. In addition to the obvious or overt influences mentioned above, we all live in a world that has a set of dominant values. Most of us don't even acknowledge these values in terms of the effect they have on how we relate to people and things around us. The influence of the world is quite subtle; it is our environment and it is difficult to see, like not being able to see the forest for the trees. Our personal frame of reference or perspective is greatly influenced by what may be called a world view of things; it is our world's frame of reference. It affects the perspective of all who live in our western culture. Ortega y Gassett (1959) describes the influence this way: "They don't know what is happening to them and that is precisely what is happening to them" (p. 119). The world view actually dominates our lives, and we don't even recognize its influence in most cases.

I think it is important to try to describe this world view of things. In German, it is called the "zeitgeist," meaning "the spirit of the times." The zeitgeist influences all things in the society: laws, business, sports, recreation, the arts, etc. Our personal values are shaped by this force; decisions made for the public good depend primarily on the zeitgeist of our world. It is the code, written and unwritten, of how we are to behave. This world view or zeitgeist is very different today than it was a century ago, and somewhat different from what it was a few decades ago. Different parts of the world have their own zeitgeist. For example, the Western world view is not the same as the prevailing world view in the Middle East or the Far East.

The zeitgeist of our Western world was initially influenced by Hebrew laws and values. The Hebrews recognized God as the supreme ruler of the universe, and their concept of what was right or wrong was dependent on what the prophets communicated to the people as the will of God. The Greeks also influenced our Western world view with their idea of more fallible gods and gave man a more direct role in determining what was right or wrong. Through the centuries, the world view has gradually evolved to one that does not have a spiritual dimension, but has man as the supreme judge of what is right or wrong. We have moved from a theocentric, or God-centred world view, to an anthropocentric or man-centred perspective. It is an anthropocentric world that prevails in our Western society; no longer is there a recognition of God as the supreme being who sets the standards for correct conduct. This anthropocentric view persists despite the fact that a large majority of people claim to believe in a deity. The Western world countries have legal systems that were initially based on a Judeo-Christian code of conduct. Now what is correct is not based on theological principles, but on what the majority of the people want to do. Often the majority, in their desire to be fair, subjugate their values to the wishes of the minorities. In many of our public schools, it is not permissible to read scriptures or to pray. As an example, in Utah and Idaho, legal battles are being fought because prayers were offered in graduation ceremonies. In Alberta, in response to parent protests, some school systems have been forced to discontinue the recitation of the Lord's prayer in classrooms. These examples of the anthropocentric world view provide evidence that what is acceptable behavior for the culture as a whole will change as society is pressured by man's opinions. This influence may also be very subtle and as Ortega y Gassett mentioned, most of us don't even know we are being influenced.

The world view that so subtly and powerfully influences us continues to impact on our schools. Earlier schools, even in this century, concentrated primarily on the academic aspect of schooling, but now schools have a much broader mandate. Schools now have tasks that belonged to the parents or the church in previous decades. I believe this is a result of the anthropocentric view of the world. The teacher's role now includes job training and socialization skills. Schools are now expected to teach students about substance abuse, human sexuality, decision-making, and a host of other social skills that other agencies outside the schools previously had as their responsibility. I do not argue with the importance of the things being taught, but rather question the schools taking over these additional responsibilities. At a time when public school teachers are asked to assume much of the moral instruction of students, it has become very difficult to determine what values should be taught. I believe the schools have been sterilized in terms of looking for any spiritual direction or in teaching students to look for spiritual help because of the prevailing anthropocentric and technological world views. Thus those values previously instilled by the church or home often go untouched by anyone. In the public school systems, there are virtually no references to things that are beyond man's ability to interpret or explain scientifically. Science and technology are expected to supplant religious views with provable scientific laws. The more I consider the forces that affect our perspective, the more I see the need for direction from a source beyond man's ever changing values.

There is a predominance of science in our world that can be seen in almost every facet of our lives. As our world view evolved, science became part of the anthropocentric world to help explain man's relationship to the universe. Technology is king, and metaphors describing man as a machine or a computer abound. Scientific research has tried to quantify man's actions and treat humans as machines capable of measured amounts of output (output being anything man does). Solway (1989) has termed this emphasis on technology and science as "le virage technologique" (p. 31). In our society's desire to rationally explain the actions of man, we have continually tried to categorize actions and analyze by statistical means the behavior of human beings. This influence is all-encompassing and forms part of our language. It is not uncommon to hear about an "interface" between two groups of people, or to speak of a student's "output" or ability to "process information." All of these terms were designed for machines. The organizations in which we work often have a technological orientation, and words like "efficient" and "effective" are very common. Efficiency and effectiveness often override human concerns when decisions are made in our businesses and even in our educational institutions. In Alberta, the Minister of Education recently published a document called *Visions for the Nineties . . . A Plan of Action* (1991) which outlines the goals and objectives of Alberta Education for the rest of this decade. By the emphasis placed on exams alone, it affirms the fact that education in this province is based on a technological model.

In education, a people profession, the technological paradigm holds sway. The act of teaching has been analyzed and reduced to methodologies or recipes. Many claim that if sufficiently practiced, these methods should lead to maximum student output. The inspiration or intuition that guides the artistic effort of the great teachers receives only token value as the science of teaching is taught to emerging teachers. Solway's (1989) statement regarding the training of education students paints a dismal picture of our newly trained teachers:

> The potential for true excellence in a young teacher may be frustrated or inhibited by the accentuation of the technological imperative. Instead of being encouraged to read, to think, to converse, to acquire mastery, he is tightly confined in his pedagogical swaddling clothes, mentally bound, and so matriculates already partially deformed. (p. 31)

As Solway's statement indicates, our new teachers have spent more time learning how to use the correct methods than they have learning the subject to which they will apply the methods. It seems very much like teaching to a recipe that may or may not work for the students mixed into the teacher's particular dish. I wonder how much more these new teachers could do for our youth if they came to us with more expertise in their subject, and the habits of pondering, evaluating, and problem-solving that they could model for their charges.

Two European scholars, Dr. Kuninski of Poland and Dr. O'Keeffe of England, while lecturing to doctoral students at Brigham Young University in the summer of 1990, criticized North American educators for being overly concerned with methodology rather than a mastery of the subject they are to teach. Comparisons of students from around the world with North American graduates on rigorous academic tests gives some credence to their argument. Undoubtedly our love of the sciences leads to our present concern about methodology. Even more so, our love of technological or scientific measures has led to North America's penchant for testing. Standardized tests, certainly not always an accurate measure of student abilities, drive the curriculum and hold teachers' curriculum ideas captive. It is testing that drives our curriculum to concern itself with the facts and skills often unconnected to the work of the mind outside of an exercise in memorization.

In considering the work of teaching and the problems our present system faces, I want to suggest that we consider education as the work of the mind and as a two-fold process. Mitchell (1985) calls the two parts the "registry" and the "commentary." The registry is the part of the mind that comprehends the information the senses gather and places the facts in the appropriate file. The commentary is where the mind takes a grasp of itself and considers the information and its place in the total scheme of things. In the commentary, we evaluate, ponder, and consider how the information helps us to solve problems.

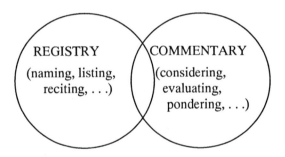

The Work of the Mind

In the commentary we go beyond comprehension to understanding.

Our concern over man's ability to measure his own progress has led us to work primarily on the registry of the mind while neglecting the mind's ability to comment on the facts and skills it acquires. This in turn adversely affects the registry itself, as it is unable to develop the relationships so necessary to the recall of information. It is little wonder that many in the business community find fault with the ability of our graduates to use the knowledge they acquire in meaningful ways. Standardized tests often encourage our teachers to teach facts independent of context. Students are not required to do much more than regurgitate answers from the materials teachers have exposed them to or drilled them on in order to prepare for the test. In many places, a teacher's competency is gauged by how well the students have memorized for the test. The sad case is that these memorized facts are fleeting bits of information; the mind knows them only as trivia and has not placed them in a schema that renders them useful in future problem solving activities. In other words, the mind has not had a chance to consider the new knowledge and how it may be useful or how it connects to the world we live in. The work of the mind involving the commentary has not been done.

I would like to suggest that our teaching and learning seriously consider developing both aspects of the work of the mind. Webb and Shute (1990) call this "predicative teaching and learning."

Predicative Teaching and Learning

Predicative teaching and learning is more a "state of mind" or "perspective" than anything else. This state of mind or perspective is so complex, so full of higher order thinking, that it is not possible to give it a finite definition, but I believe it is safe to say that it goes against the grain of the current world view. Lauren Resnick (1987) writes about higher order thinking as something difficult to define, yet something that is easy to recognize when it is seen. I want to consider a few things that I feel could be recognized as predicative teaching and learning.

A disposition toward predicative teaching and learning is not easily acquired. One cannot learn it in a few lessons and practice sessions. It requires a great deal of reading and a lot of thinking about what one reads. It requires time to personalize the concept. I don't believe that predicative teaching and learning is a concept that can be taught in the conventional sense of teaching. It is an experience. Teachers may be coached, guided, or even prodded as they develop the mindset or perspective of predicative teaching and learning, but it always comes from great individual effort. This is illustrated by Gibboney (1991) when he points out the impossibility of a teacher putting knowledge into the mind of a student. He says:

> . . . a teacher cannot give an idea directly to a student. What the student gets is facts dressed up as an idea. This is so because we truly get an idea by wrestling with it on our own in a situation that has some purpose or meaning to us, that elicits some engagement of the imagination and emotion as well as the mind. The student must figure it out with the help of the teacher and other students in an environment that is rich in materials and activities that give access to community and regional life. (p. 683)

The understanding of predicative teaching comes through a personalization process involving extensive reading, discussion, and writing. I believe it is through writing that the concept becomes the clearest, and if it isn't written about, it may not be personalized sufficiently to become a perspective or a mindset. Many authors, including Mitchell, state that the consideration of knowledge is accomplished best in writing. Mitchell (1985) says ". . . the mind does its most important work through the consideration and manipulation of language" (p. 6). C. Day Lewis wrote, "We do not write in order to be understood, we write in order to understand" (p. 15). While I believe writing is one of the best ways to personalize knowledge and develop the commentary, I know it may be accomplished effectively through other expressive or interpretive activities. Artists of all persuasions go through a personalization process when doing their work. Teachers also develop the commentary in the preparation for teaching and in the act of teaching. Predicative teaching and learning understands this work of the mind and models it in and out of the classroom.

The development of the perspective or frame of reference that becomes predicative teaching and learning requires that information gathered from our experiences in life, especially through reading, be reflected upon. We must try to see the perplexities and struggle through them in search of the meaning which fits our own "weltangshuung" or personal view of the world.

Predicative teaching is the deliberate attempt to have a student take hold of the information he acquires, and then work it over carefully in his mind, considering its usefulness and possible applications. This process of considering, pondering, and evaluating allows the mind to do more than comprehend the information; it allows a person to understand the knowledge he has stored away and, in fact, allows his mind to more accurately file and cross-reference the information for future use. This idea is not uncommon, but its practice is. I believe we need to change our practice of teaching by giving greater consideration to both parts of the mind, the registry and the commentary.

Brown (1988) points out there is a call for a change in our teaching and learning; it is widespread and comes from many reputable sources. A big percentage of those who call for change tell us that we need to have students better able to think. Many people have tried to respond to the call for changes, but many times the call is answered by a recipe for success that some individual has found works in his or her particular setting. Program usefulness in each setting must be questioned, and too often isn't because we look for the quick fix. Programs that try to change our schools for the better all too often involve a plan to raise test scores, and thus give us more schooling of the technological variety. When we have a mindset concerned with predicative teaching and learning, we will be leery of any prescriptive programs or activities in the classroom, especially those to develop better thinking skills. Predicative teaching and learning is not solely about skills and information, it is about pondering and considering. This higher order thinking Resnick (1987) calls a mysterious activity. It is not a simple or even a complex skill which can be taught. Predicative teaching and learning is the perspective that comes from always carefully considering the experiences that we have and our own unique background in making sense of the world.

Predicative teaching and learning requires an initial presentation of information that the student comprehends and is able to store in his or her memory for future or immediate consideration. We need information in the mind for consideration, but putting in the information is a much simpler task than promoting the thought processes which lead to understanding. The teacher in his preparations must understand these ideas about learning so he can give serious thought to the planning of learning activities that encourage or require a student to ponder and consider the information acquired in class.

Shute and Webb (1989) claim that it is through the act of teaching that the best personalization of knowledge, and therefore real learning, takes place. It is a test to see if we have personalized the information well enough to teach it. "Docemur docendo," he who teaches learns. We must work in the commentary of the mind if we are to teach, and doing this should ensure an understanding of what we teach. A recent study revealed that students who studied material thinking they would be required to teach it to others, even though they did not, scored significantly higher on tests than students who did not anticipate teaching. The research also showed that students who prepared to teach, and then actually taught, significantly outscored those students who only prepared to teach. Shute and Webb (1989) state:

> An educational pattern that takes advantage of the teaching to learn process has two elements. First, learners acquire knowledge. Second, they expand on or transform that knowledge. Expanding or transforming one's knowledge structures is a means of giving personal meaning to one's learning. We contend that teaching to learn is a superior way to personalize learning. (p. 31)

Sometimes it is tempting to think that thoughtfulness or the ability to ponder and reflect is a skill or function which is found in only the elite rather than in all learners. Lauren Resnick (1987) makes this statement in contradiction of that notion: "Higher order thinking is the hallmark of successful learning at all levels – not only the more advanced" (p. 45). Even the little child can develop the virtue of thoughtfulness.

In predicative teaching and learning, there is a desire to promote student questions and to think of truly educated persons as those who ask questions after doing some thinking of their own. An educated person is someone who has developed what Solway (1989) calls the "interrogative" mind. This would be modeled by the teacher, learning with the students and ponders out loud.

Dillon (1988) describes the importance of the interrogative mind that a predicative teacher would strive to encourage and develop:

> ...perplexity. That is the precondition of questioning and thus the prerequisite of learning. . . . Perplexity does not occur of itself. It is the main event of the moment but not the first. At the very start there is some precept, P. Next we introduce P into our scheme of things – other P's in our organized experience. When our scheme does not readily accommodate P, we have a disjunction between the new P_1 and selected previous ones, P_2. The experience of perplexity ensues, whereupon a question may arise. (p. 18)

This perplexity, which brings about a question, comes from the process of personalization that a teacher encourages by promoting student questions which go beyond the clarification level. The discussion of an issue by students in a classroom enhances the personalization process and promotes further perplexities in all students who get involved. Dillon tells us as teachers to ask only questions that perplex self. In this way, the teacher models predicative learning for students.

Predicative teaching and learning requires us to look at some tasks of teaching in many different ways. Assessment of learning must also be thoughtfully done in predicative teaching and learning. The teacher who understands the work of the mind as a two-part process recognizes the need to do more than ask for facts from the student's registry of information. It is important that students acquire facts, and it is easy to design a test to see how well they have memorized, but thinking about the information is what a predicative teacher wants to see. This thinking about what has been learned may be assessed by the questions students ask, by writing, or some other exhibition of thoughtfulness. Wiggins (1989) calls this "authentic testing." This type of testing goes beyond recall or testing the registry, to testing a person's understanding of the subject. One good demonstration of understanding would be having students successfully teach others, and then do their own evaluation of what they had taught. This exercise requires a great deal more than comprehension on the part of the student who teaches. Likely the most common way to have students demonstrate how well they understand something is to have them write about it. As we write we must sort out our thoughts and perhaps allow the mind to take a grasp of itself (Mitchell, 1985). Problem-solving is another common way to allow students to demonstrate their understanding of material they have studied. In predicative teaching and learning, the teacher is concerned with both the registry and the commentary, and tests or evaluation procedures would reflect that understanding.

Predicative teaching and learning is the antithesis of the technological mindset which pervades our world. Ellen Langer (1989) describes the thoughtlessness that results from this technological outlook on life and calls it "mindlessness." Mindlessness sets in when we rely too rigidly on categories and distinctions created in the past. We act automatically, without thinking, using these ready-made categories. A teacher who is concerned with predicative teaching and learning will be the opposite of the mindlessness that Langer describes and be open and thoughtful. Langer describes three characteristics of a mindful person, and these are also characteristic of the predicative teacher and learner. First, the mindful person is open to new information. Second, as new information is acquired, the mindful person can make shifts in the categories the mind uses to file information. Last, Langer says the mindful person tries hard to have multiple categories for information he acquires. Teachers with a predicative teaching and learning perspective will encourage these characteristics in their students and in themselves. Developing this mindfulness, we become more aware of the things that influence us. We act thoughtfully rather than reacting to the world we live in.

The predicative teacher is aware of the zeitgeist or world view that permeates the world, and is able to develop his own weltangshuung or perspective that will drive him, even in the face of the overwhelming technological mindset that Solway (1989) calls "le virage technologique" (p. 31). It is critical that the teacher be aware of the effects of the predominant world view in order to effectively work against it and not be taken along in its powerful current.

It requires a major effort in terms of reading, discussing, writing, and pondering to build up a reservoir of new understandings which can help us see a world perspective that is primarily technologically oriented. This technological orientation has permeated almost all of us to the point where it is most difficult to think critically instead of analytically. By analytically, I mean the mindless categorization of information. Instead of really thinking about something in terms of its meaning for us, we simply find an appropriate bin in our minds for information we receive. This is where discussing and writing about what we have read becomes critically important. The search for correct words to express ourselves requires a form of personalization, and in doing this, we allow ourselves to move from a level of comprehension to a level of understanding. We need to give our students time to think about what they learn and then time for them to talk to others about what they learn (Raths et al 1986).

The technological mindset has been with us for many years, and writers early in this century recognized the trend towards thoughtlessness that now prevails in our society. Whitehead (1929) spoke of the encroachment of this mindlessness in lectures he delivered around 1913. Ortega y Gassett (1944) described the problems he saw in Spain when the scientific or technological perspective became predominant in his country and in the world. Today Ortega y Gassett's predictions have proven to be correct, and scientific or technological views in education provide ample proof. The thoughtfulness of many people is curtailed by society's desire to quantify everything. The problem with the quantification of knowledge is that it becomes an end in itself for many people. Sigmund Freud (1937) said:

> We know that the first step towards the intellectual mastery of the world in which we live is the discovery of general principles, rules, and laws which bring order into chaos. By such mental operations we simplify the world of phenomena, but we cannot avoid falsifying it in doing so, especially when we are dealing with processes of development and change. (p. 228)

Writers in the past few years point to the same problem. Solway (1989) said much the same thing as Freud:

> My central argument is that the technological paradigm is destructive because, in its indiscriminate application to the human situation, it violates the laws of intellectual and imaginative development. (p. 106)

A predicative teacher and learner heeds the warnings of these writers. He ponders thoughtfully the force of mindlessness that always encroaches upon his considerations.

Understanding predicative teaching and learning takes a long time. It takes time to develop thoughtful habits in teaching. It takes time and effort to successfully model perplexity and thoughtful questions for students. It takes time and effort to move from a level of comprehension to a level of understanding. (We must read about, write about, discuss, and teach predication.) It takes time to learn about the predominant world view and to assess our own views. It takes time, but with time comes the experience needed to understand predicative teaching and learning. Understanding predicative teaching and learning gives us that special perspective necessary to really help learners develop the mind.

Toni Kennedy is a resource teacher for the Calgary Board of Education, identifying students with exceptional needs, and mentoring teachers. Toni graduated with a B.A. in Sociology from the University of Hawaii, a B.Ed. from the University of Calgary, and a M.A. in Administration from Gonzaga University. She is presently coauthoring a teacher education textbook for use in post-secondary institutions. Toni is involved in organizing many professional development activities for the teachers in her school system. Her seven-year-old daughter, Jessica, has played an important role in Toni's journey toward thoughtfulness.

2

Thoughtfulness Makes Me Tense

Toni Kennedy

It must be nearly 3:00 this Saturday afternoon and I, as usual, am hunched over my computer, fingers poised on the keyboard, and eyes staring at what seems a forever blank screen. My inner voice is playing coach and is nudging me to think, pull it together, and just start. But the din of my daughter playing with her friend is too much and I cannot concentrate. From the computer room, I shout "Jessica, I am trying to work. Please be quiet." An immediate hush falls but my attention is now centred on the conversation my daughter is having with her playmate. The playmate queries, "What is your mom doing?" Jessica accurately responds, "She's working on an assignment." "What's an assignment?" questions her playmate. "She's writing about thoughtfulness," replies my daughter. Her playmate pushes her further and asks, "What is thoughtfulness?" After a long pause, my daughter confesses, "I don't know, but it sure makes her tense."

This chapter will focus on my personal journey towards thoughtfulness. Before sharing my journey, I must clarify what I mean by "thoughtfulness" and herein lies my dilemma. For the term thoughtfulness conjures within me great perplexity. Perhaps it is this perplexity that is indeed thoughtfulness. Webster (1988) defines thinking as the process of arranging ideas in a pattern of relationships or of adding new ideas soon to be related to such a pattern; to turn something over in the mind e.g. to consider advantages and disadvantages. Thought is defined as the action or process of thinking, the capacity to think. Thoughtful too is defined as being absorbed in the process of thought, showing consideration for others. Mitchell (1985) speaks of thoughtfulness as the ability of the mind to grasp itself. To further explain this, visualize the mind as being two distinct circles. The first circle is the registry. This is where all knowledge is stored. Hirsch (1988) would see the registry as possessing the basic information needed to thrive in the modern world. The second circle is the considering or understanding part of the mind. Thoughtfulness can only be realized when through inquiry or perplexity, the considering part of the mind contemplates what is in the registry. It is here when the mind has truly taken grasp of itself that thoughtfulness can be recognized. Thoughtfulness then is the opportunity for people to think about what they place and what they possess in the registry. Hooke (1665) further clarifies the idea of thoughtfulness. He elucidates, "It is the great prerogative of Mankind above other creatures, that we are not only able to behold the works of Nature . . . but we have also the power of considering [and] comparing them . . . "

But how is this dormant disposition of thoughtfulness awakened within the thoughts of mankind? History testifies through its apocalyptic nature that the disposition of thoughtfulness is latent and often lies fallow generation after generation. Within my personal growth over the years, there has been the occasional stirring or perhaps even the germination of thoughtfulness, but alas, as is usual in a school setting, the seedling is often pulled from the security of the soil to check the health of its roots until its inevitable death. As a teacher I am often in wonderment along with my students, but modelling is a powerful tool, and I am sadly confident that I suffocated many of my students by far too often examining their roots at the expense of never experiencing their blooms.

My mind, ever so gingerly, began to take the grasp of itself when I became aware in 1984 that I was experiencing the miracle of being the host to the creation of another life. My disposition of thoughtfulness sky-rocketed to the forefront with a neophyte at the controls. Perplexity, followed by a thirst for knowledge to find out why and how this life was growing, led me to book after book which incited within me more questions and more searches for answers, only to discover more questions. My grade four students journeyed with me through this wonderful enlightened time. And, often with many little loving hands inquisitively and strategically placed upon my swollen tummy, we dialogued and philosophized about the wonderment of life. Socrates would have been proud! My students and I were blooming and their roots were secure. My students, of course, moved on to someone else, and one would think that nine-year-olds have short memories, but every so often I have the serendipitous pleasure of meeting one of them and testimony validates that something special did indeed happen.

One can get careless, though, and over the next six years my quest for new questions and answers resulted in the pursuit of a master's degree, some that was acceptingly a tabula rasa[1] nature, and some that involved the process of collaboration, which perhaps did not blossom forth into thoughtfulness, but at least the roots were being allowed to strengthen and reach for unknown depths. A child, a newly acquired master's degree, a challenging position within the school system, and acceptance into a doctoral program. Life was indeed splendid! At this time too, I had the opportunity to meet a courageous young lady of fourteen named Melissa. My own child taught me about the wonders of life; Melissa taught me about the disdain of death.

Melissa was tiny, barely four foot eight, and yet in her presence one soon became aware that her character towered over the tallest. Her battle with life started at conception. Her mother was an alcoholic and gave little regard for the nurturing of this precious life. At age five, Melissa was dealt another cruel blow when she was diagnosed as having juvenile arthritis. As the disease progressed, her joints stiffened to the extent that when she walked she was only able to shuffle, and often the ravages of pain were evident in her doll-like face. School was not easy for Melissa either. Her classmates were often cruel, making fun of her unstylish clothes and unkempt hair. Some of her teachers referred to her as lazy and accused her of using her disease as an excuse not to work. I came to know and grew to love Melissa at this juncture in her life. I could not understand why a child had to suffer so; and then life began to change for Melissa. She was placed in yet another foster home, but this one seemed different. Her classmates and her teachers simultaneously began providing her with warmth. Melissa was flourishing. Her pain had seemed to ease somewhat because she was receiving consistent therapy and her shuffle was conveying the message of optimism. Life was indeed wonderful. And then on May 3, 1990, Melissa died. Her taxi driver stumbled while carrying her down the school steps, and the brunt of his fall was absorbed by Melissa's head. I held her hand and watched her die. Thoughtfulness surged to the forefront within me again, but this time the ghost of a little girl was at the helm. Her death left me with many unanswered questions, some of which will remain elusive until my own departure, but her death will not go without meaning. Melissa's death has brought about a lifelong commitment from me to pursue for all children a safe learning environment – one that not only encourages the work of the mind, but one which will allow the work of the mind to be carried on in a thoughtful environment. Brown (1987) further substantiates the idea: "Leadership in public schools means, essentially, providing the *setting* and the *incentives* for doing thoughtfully and humanely the work of the mind" (p.49). It is with these two events, the birth of a child and the death of a child, that thoughtfulness was beginning to awaken within me. My journey had just begun.

It was in this frame of mind that I arrived at the campus of Brigham Young University (BYU). I soon learned that before thoughtfulness can occur, it is necessary to be able to capture knowledge. Webb and Shute (1987) believe the aim of the student is to be able to gain complete and accurate understanding of what the teacher or the text is trying to convey. They explain:

> Such understanding precedes higher-order, expanded thinking – the ultimate desideratum. Just as we cannot depart, geographically, from a place unless we are there to begin with, so we cannot expand our knowledge of an idea unless we first understand it clearly. (p. 31)

It became imperative for me not only to comprehend the written word, but to comprehend and listen to the spoken word. Covey (1985) describes this as developing the habit of empathic listening. He defines empathic listening as "getting inside another person's frame of reference. You look out through it, you see the world the way they see the world, you understand their paradigm, you understand how they feel" (p. 240). Once you truly understand then you can seek to be understood. Cory (1988) explicates:

> You are not engaged so much in acquiring knowledge as in making mental efforts under criticism. . . . A certain amount of knowledge you can indeed with average faculties acquire so as to retain; nor need you regret the hours you spend on much that is forgotten, for the shadow of lost knowledge at least protects you from many illusions. But you go to a great school not so much for knowledge as for arts and habits; for the habit of attention, for the art of expression, for the art of assuming at a moment's notice a new intellectual position, for the art of entering quickly into another person's thoughts, for the habit of submitting to censure and refutation, for the art of indicating assent or dissent in graduated terms, for the habit of regarding minute points of accuracy, for the art of working out what is possible in a given time . . . for discrimination, for mental courage and mental soberness. And above all you go to a great school for self-knowledge. (p.10)

Self-knowledge is my aspiration and I look forward to continuing the process of educating me.

Once having captured the knowledge and considered it, one too must be able to express it. Mitchell (1981) infers that writing is thinking manifest. What a profound assertion! How many of my fellow teachers have requested help for putting their thoughts into words? Teachers have graduated from high school and then on to a four year university program and still some cannot put together the simplest of curriculum newsletters. Is their thinking so muddled they can not express themselves?

Solway (1989) relates the anecdote of how he was marking his college students' papers with his house guest, a celebrated and distinguished chess grandmaster, peering over his shoulder. His guest remarked, "I didn't know you taught at a school for retarded students" (p. 57). Solway reflects:

> I realized immediately that my guest was not being facetious. . . .His own high intelligence may have rendered him somewhat intolerant of substandard material, but at the same time he had in one brief observation placed the problem I faced in a new and perhaps accurate perspective. It was not the sort of thing one would say at a departmental meeting or pedagogical seminar . . . but it summed up the facts of the case with unsentimental clarity. (p. 57)

Solway continues that he did no more marking that day but rather walked and reconsidered his professional commitment. I too am beginning to think.

Mitchell's statement that writing is thinking manifest has caused me great bewilderment. If the students we are graduating cannot write, are we as members of the public education system failing? If the graduates of universities have difficulty manifesting their thinking, are universities failing? Is it necessary to point to where the fault lies? What is my role or any teacher's role in addressing this need? Questions and more questions which lead to reflective thinking, dialoguing with colleagues, and more reading. Is this another testimony for the recognition of thoughtfulness within myself?

Striving for thoughtfulness is hard work – maybe that is why it readily accepts to lie dormant within the heart of man. Dr. Kuninski, a visiting scholar from Poland, bluntly stated that in order for learning to take place, suffering must be experienced. "Suffering"[2]– at the mere utterance of the word we gasped in horror. Surely this word was used in error, but upon requests for clarification, the word remained the same. Suffering, surely only someone with a Communist background would equate learning with suffering. How could this be? It was happening again, in the quiet times of my mind suffering would loom and I would begin to think. The "suffering" haunting caused me to reflect upon the many conversations I have had over the years with my now octogenarian father concerning finances. Each time this inevitable conversation would occur, my father would clarify for me that if something were given readily it would not ever have the same value as something that has had to be earned or a sacrifice made for its attainment. Is this what Kuninski meant, that real learning must involve suffering? I watch my daughter, now in grade two, learning to communicate in French. It is hard and sometimes there are even tears, and I suspect, suffering, but she is earning her learning. Is suffering synonymous with levelling up the academic expectations of our students? When Gradillas[3] passionately delivers his plea for providing not only equal opportunity but equal expectations for students, I feel certain that he would concur there must be some suffering. I am confident that if I were to speak to any of Escalante's[4] students, they would readily relate to suffering. As a doctoral student, I certainly know about suffering. Upon the mere mention of the word "thoughtful," my brain seems to swell to headache proportions, the eyes squint, the muscles in the neck and shoulders tighten, and I start to suffer, but like my daughter, I am earning my learning.

While earning my learning that first summer on my doctorate program, another puzzle piece was presented to me which provided a gentle nudge toward thoughtfulness. Dr. DeLong lectured our class on the transformation of leadership. He eloquently led us somewhat whimsically down "the yellow brick road," using all the right quotations and validations. I remember being almost lulled into academic euphoria and then I was hurled into reality with the following anecdote. His brother is involved with the rescue of skiers who are caught in avalanches. He asked us to imagine what it must be like to hear that deathly roar of tons and tons of snow cascading down a mountainside and to feel the flinging and hurling of your body against the mountain. And then, total disorientation, to hear nothing but the pounding of your heart in a suffocating white coffin and to claw in panic, not knowing which way is up, for the breath of life that often never comes. It was here in the story he told of the sadness his brother often encountered. Many corpses of the young and robust have been found only a few inches from the surface, the skiers in confusion and in desperation for life having clawed in the wrong direction. If the skiers had but thought for a moment, they could have saved their own lives. Suffocating in a white tomb, the skiers need only to have spit. The gravitational pull on the spit would have oriented the position and provided a map to the surface. Spit! It all seemed so simple, just spit!

Dr. DeLong's illustration emphasizes the value of practising proactivity – living in the now, always thinking big, but starting with a small win. Proactivity means that "as human beings, we are responsible for our own lives. Our behavior is a function of our decisions, not our conditions" (Covey, 1985, p. 71). Questioning, inquiry, perplexity, exploration, scrutiny, and it was all clinging to spit! The gentle nudge had become a piercing jab as once more I was compelled to think. Can you imagine a classroom guided by a proactive teacher and the power of that modelling for the students in this classroom? Can you imagine a room full of students licensed with the power to be proactive? Would thoughtfulness more readily occur?

And so for me, my journey towards thoughtfulness continues. Like the skier caught in the avalanche, I now possess the knowledge to know which direction I must travel in my search for thoughtfulness. To bring wonder into my personal life and to model wonder in my professional life and to celebrate wonder when I recognize it in my family, friends, colleagues, and students is an ambition for which I will labor. The fleeting awakenings of thoughtfulness within myself that I have shared throughout this essay confirm for me that becoming thoughtful is not a linear process, but rather a process of expansion that can at times even collapse upon itself, but once recognized, it cannot be lost. Thoughtfulness generates perplexity, and there is nothing easy about being perplexed. To be thoughtful requires effort and unadorned hard work and yes, thoughtfulness can even make one tense.

Notes

[1] Tabula rasa is the perception that learners are to be viewed as empty vessels. The teacher's role is to fill the empty vessels with knowledge. In order to determine whether or not the vessel is being filled, tests which rely heavily on memorization are given. Looking at Mitchell's model of the mind, the registry would be the empty vessel portion of the brain. It is my belief that learners must possess certain knowledge in order to contemplate, but when a teacher views his or her job as only to impart information, and if the learner views his or her job as only to collect information, then real learning is not happening.

[2] The word "suffering" still holds a tremendous amount of emotion for my colleagues. When this portion of the essay was presented to my cohort group, debate and what I would like to call "thoughtful" discussion ensued. Although feeling somewhat like the villain in a fantasy, I do not wish to remove this scenario because for me, the use of the word "suffering" in relationship to learning has caused me a great deal of perplexity. After our Saturday marathon of higher educational activity, I conclude it has caused perplexity for my colleagues also.

According to Webster (1988), suffering is defined as physical or mental pain, distress, loss, damage, etc. "To suffer" is defined as being made to bear, to put up with, to undergo, to be made subject to. It is my belief that Dr. Kuninski does not intend that our classrooms be dungeons of horror where learning can happen only when one is placed on the rack. But I believe that he envisions real learning to be taking place in an environment that challenges students, one in which the students' full potential is targeted, and one in which the students take responsibility for their learning. I think the kind of suffering he refers to is similar to what a runner in a marathon race must subject himself to in order to be a finisher. "Suffering," I believe, can be equated with "effortful." Effort on the part of the students is required in order for their optimum potential to be reached. Resnick (1987), when listing some of the key features of higher order thinking, states, "Higher order thinking is effortful. There is considerable mental work involved in the kinds of elaborations and judgments required" (p. 3). In other words, learning takes a lot of hard work. Smith (1990) opposes this position and differentiates between easy and hard learning by saying that hard learning is contrived and is difficult when it is deliberate and intentional. He further elaborates that, "Learning that is driven by determination and effort is paradoxically likely to be the least efficient learning of all" (p. 40). I have difficulty with Smith's explanation here. Perhaps the argument involves whose determination is at stake for learning to take place. If I decide or contrive someone's learning, I can see his point. It is the proverbial "you-can-lead-a-horse-to-water-but-you-cannot-make-him-drink" syndrome. But if the student accepts the responsibility for the learning, I still contend that it is effortful. Walking, for a young child, appears to be learned in an effortless way, and yet my observations of my daughter learning to walk validates for me that learning to walk requires a great deal of effort and even causes frustration at times. This is the fallacy in Smith's comments. When someone has at last mastered a task, it appears effortless, but in order for the facade of effortlessness to be observed, great effort on the part of the learner has taken place. Schools, I believe, have been focusing on what appears to be the effortlessness of one who exhibits success. Tomlinson and Cross (1991) report:

> ... schools and reformers have vigorously searched for school improvements that would boost academic achievement without necessarily requiring additional effort from the students themselves. ... many of their efforts ... were counter productive; for example, reduced or abolished core course requirements, and greater discretion for students in their choices of courses as well as the terms of their agreement to behave in class and try to learn. All of these practices and policies made school easier, of course, and graduation rates rose in response. But they did not make it easier by improving school quality. Rather, they did it by making it easier to avoid hard work and difficult courses. (p. 70)

Tomlinson and Cross (1991) citing Csikszemtmihalyi (1990) note his observations that "the chief impediments to literacy are not cognitive in nature. It is not that students can't learn; it is that they do not wish to learn" (p. 70). Students are not taking responsibility for their learning, nor are they showing any indication that they are willing to put effort into their learning. Tomlinson and Cross (1991) citing Mullis et al (1990) relate:

> ... 71 percent of our high school seniors study for one hour a day or less and just 10 percent spend more than two hours a day on homework. Similarly, 62 percent of our 8th graders and 56 percent of our high school seniors read 10 or fewer pages a day in all their classes together. (p. 70)

Students, then, must be prepared to be subjected to effortfulness or mental "suffering" in order for real learning to take place. Brown (1988) concurs:

> ... it's one of those kinds of pain that is easily forgotten, as when we've finally figured out a puzzle or when, after all the digging and planting and weeding and worrying, the crop comes in, looking and tasting just as we imagined it would. (p. 6)

I conclude that we all earn our learning.

[3]Henry Gradillas, a former graduate of BYU, was a guest lecturer there in the summer of 1990. Dr. Gradillas had been the principal of Garfield High School in East Los Angeles. Mathews (1988) describes Garfield High School in the following manner:

> At least 80 percent of Garfield High School students qualify for the federal free or reduced-price lunch program, which means their annual incomes fall below $15 000 for a family of four. At least 25 percent of the students come from families that receive Aid to Families with Dependent Children, and that figure would probably be much larger if so many of the poor were not illegal aliens afraid to seek any government help. ... More than 95 percent of the Garfield student body is Latino. Some of the families have recently immigrated to the United Stated from Mexico, often illegally. Even long-term residents usually speak Spanish at home. Few of the homes have many books

in any language, or framed degrees on the wall from institutions of any kind. (p. 2-3)

It was during Gradillas' time of administration that Garfield High School in 1982 produced more Advanced Placement Calculus students than all but three public schools in the country. Dr. Gradillas opened the doors which allowed for this excellence to happen. In his lecture to us, Gradillas shared the idea that he feels that the biggest problem happening in schools is that they do not expect enough of the students. He believes that *all* students should be challenged and that learning is hard work. He believes that students fail because of low expectations. He validates this by citing that when the teachers of Garfield High began changing their mindset about the students, then success had a chance to happen.

[4]Jaime Escalante, the most celebrated teacher at Garfield High School, was the calculus teacher of the students who passed the Advanced Placement calculus examination. He is the focus of the book *Escalante: The Best Teacher in America* written by Jay Mathews. He also is the heart of the movie *Stand and Deliver*.

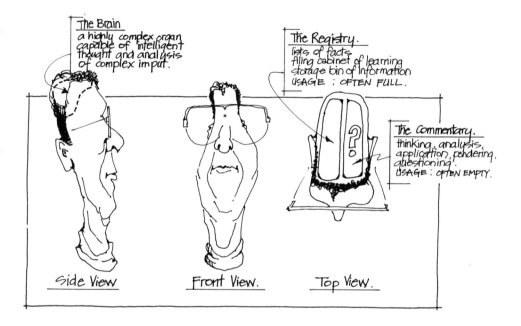

The Brain
a highly complex organ
capable of intelligent
thought and analysis
of complex imput.

The Registry.
lists of facts
filing cabinet of learning
storage bin of information
USAGE : OFTEN FULL.

The Commentary.
thinking, analysis,
application, pondering,
questioning.
USAGE : OFTEN EMPTY.

Side View   Front View.   Top View.

Peter Darby was born in Sherwood Forest in Nottingham, England. After growing up in that area of the world, he completed his initial college preparation for teaching at Westminster College, Oxford, and taught school in Africa and England before moving to Canada in 1970. He earned a B.Ed. and a M.Ed. in geography at the University of Calgary. His teaching experience in Canada has been in the public schools in central Alberta, where he has been a vice-principal and a principal as well as a classroom teacher. He is currently Assistant Superintendent of Schools (Secondary) for the County of Red Deer. He and his wife Linda, who also is a teacher, are the parents of four sons.

3

A Journey to Thoughtfulness

Peter Darby

Educators need to understand the meaning and importance of thoughtfulness. This is unlikely to happen as the result of any single event, but is more likely to occur as the result of a quest or journey to seek thoughtfulness. Richard Mitchell creates a powerful metaphor for understanding thoughtfulness when he describes the organization of the mind. This involves two areas: knowledge, such as names and dates, is captured in one area called the "registry," while reflecting or considering occurs in an area called the "commentary" (Mitchell, 1985). Thoughtfulness occurs when information which is in the registry is examined or manipulated in the commentary. This should involve not just questioning, but also striving to answer questions as personal meaning is sought. This is the mind taking a "grasp of itself" (Mitchell, 1985, p. 4). Seeking personal meaning requires inquiry in an environment which is humane, safe, and encouraging of risk-taking.

"Thoughtlessness prevails in most schools in America" (Shute, 1990). This is as a result of an absence of understanding of how the mind works and also a failure to understand the purpose of schooling. Most of the work done in our schools involves the filling of the registry, while very little time or attention is given to personalizing, questioning, or making personal meaning of what is in the registry. For example, the biology teacher tells the students the list of terms they are to learn, and then gives them a test to see if they know them. Too often the student is perceived as an empty vessel into which the teacher is supposed to pour the knowledge. Occasionally the teacher taps the vessel to see if the knowledge is still there. The knowledge is supposed to return to the teacher relatively unchanged from the information put in by the teacher. This contrasts with learning environments where the student acquires knowledge from teachers, students, books, and other media then reflects or considers the information before displaying or communicating information with others.

Where does the journey begin? A journey to thoughtfulness, unlike normal journeys, does not have an end or a beginning which is easily recognized. Thoughtfulness is an unending quest, and most of us cannot recollect our earliest mental activities or cerebrations. As each step of my journey cannot be remembered, I have chosen to describe four episodes or phases of my journey to thoughtfulness which demonstrate the impact of changing paradigms in my life. I have not always seen the world around me in the same way. As I am concerned about the future of schools, I conclude with a short journey into the future of education.

Awareness

Nothing in school seemed to prompt much thought until an errant rugby boot caught me in the ankle and changed my life. I was fourteen years old, in England, living a fairly typical untroubled and relatively mindless teenage existence. Nothing in life seemed too hard, and nothing seemed very important. The days between Monday and Friday were school days and Saturday was a day of sport which, in the winter, meant a game of rugby football in the morning and a game of soccer in the afternoon. That kick in the ankle not only made me miss my soccer game, it made me a candidate for emergency surgery to remove diseased bone, turned my father's hair grey, and gave me four weeks in a hospital bed with nothing much to do except reflect on my situation and my future. I cannot remember being really perplexed for any length of time before my stay in hospital, but many great and important questions about life passed through my head as I was forced to lie in a hospital bed. Although there were no immediate simple solutions to my questions, a drive and resolve to learn emerged in my mind which propelled me through the rest of my teenage years.

I have considered the many years I spent in the state-run schools of England and searched my mind for examples when thoughtfulness was demanded. Throughout my elementary education, I can only remember being required to recall lists of things which had been placed in the registry. This continued during my secondary education at a grammar school until I completed General Certificate of Education Ordinary Level examinations (O Levels). Then I believe I crossed the watershed into an educational environment where the work of the mind was required. I remember very clearly the words of my history teacher as we started work in history for the General Certificate of Education Advanced Level (A Level). He said that for O Levels, we had been required to show that we knew the facts, and that this was the basis for the awarding of marks. Now for the A Levels, it would be assumed that we knew the facts and would receive no marks for supplying them. Rather, we would be required to use the facts to support argument, reason, comparison, and analysis. Our marks would be awarded on the basis of how well we reasoned our position.

I found this very difficult and frustrating. It was as if I had suddenly walked from one room into another, and there did not seem to be any transition or preparation for the change. These things had not been expected before, and it seemed as if the things I had spent years learning to do, such as reciting, regurgitating, and recalling, suddenly had no value. I began to feel like a failure

were not taught to challenge answers.
Transition from high school to postsecondar

were use to having / to memorise

at school, because I no longer knew how to work successfully. What had *we*
brought success previously was no longer acceptable. *are taught in*

a manner

I also remember that almost all evaluation in the last two years of grammar
school consisted of essays, essays, essays. All assignments were essays, and *that*
every exam included essays. Questions asked you to explain, describe, contrast, *discourse*
and discuss. This was a challenge. Those who knew how to express their *not use*
thoughts in words did well, while many people who did not understand what *to have*
was being asked of them were told they were not good at school. I never saw *to*
a multiple choice exam throughout my years in state schools in England. Such *provefod.*
exams were unheard of, and I knew no one who had written one.

Exploration

My three years studying education at Oxford and two years teaching in
Africa were years of exploration of the human existence. Life in Oxford was
considerably different than life in Zambia, but there was a lot to learn in both
places. My time in Oxford I remember as a time of great reflection. I was away
from home, independent, and making my own decisions. I enjoyed the
challenges and the expectation that I would work as a scholar. College life was
exciting and I felt good about my successes, which spurred me on to greater
efforts. The atmosphere seemed to reek of studying and learning, yet several
of my classmates failed. They chose the social scene, with its demanding hours
and neglect of studies.

My decision to volunteer to teach overseas was a significant outcome of
my time at Oxford. I decided to teach overseas as a volunteer and applied to
Volunteer Services Overseas after some reflection and pondering. Getting
accepted was not easy. The interview panel sat in a horseshoe arrangement in
an intimidating room in London. The questioning was extensive and acceptance
was not automatic. I was excited to be accepted, and then rushed to look in an
atlas to find out where Zambia was located in Africa. I was assigned to teach
boys and girls at a secondary boarding school on a Salvation Army Mission
station 80 miles into the bush from the nearest city. I had never attended any
Salvation Army institution prior to working in Africa.

I remember one question that perplexed me and to which I gave considerable thought while I was in Africa: What would I do if there were a revolution
or invasion? This was an item of frequent concern as the white Rhodesians to
the south had unilaterally declared their independence, and there were frequent
rumors of an impending invasion of Zambia. I concluded that if there were a
major social upheaval, then the ordinary African living in a hut with little, if
any, knowledge of English and even less knowledge of our "civilized" ways
was the person who would care for a fellow human being far better than the

urban African. What was it that attracted me to the ordinary African? Why did I think his life was better?

Traditional African education and values support a life style that is always close to the question of the continuity of life. Details of birth, puberty, and marriage are important to learn and are well taught. At puberty even relatively well educated girls still consent to coating their bodies with mud and lying in a mud hut for weeks while they are "fattened" to increase their value in marriage. Life may be short, but it is highly valued, cherished, and nourished by everyone in the community.

The World View Accepted

All of us subscribe to a world view or a way of seeing life around us, but few of us understand what we are seeing. The world view is "so internalized that it goes unquestioned" (Rifkin, 1989, p. 19). This frame of reference is an organization of events in life that helps people feel that they understand what is happening. Our society is driven by a zeitgeist, or world view, which is based on the views of Newton, Descartes, and Bacon (Rifkin, 1989, p. 25). In this world view, man is the centre and focus of all that we do, and science and technology are dominant. This is a secular and humanistic world view that denies the existence of God. There have been times in the history of this world when other significantly different world views have prevailed. Before Christ, in the world of the Hebrews, the centre and focus of life was God, while to the ancient Greeks, the cosmos replaced God as the focus. Society has arrived at a focus on man, aided by the science and technology which has grown in dominance in the last three hundred years. It is my contention that most people, while being influenced by the mindset of the world, are unaware of the zeitgeist that they are following. Ortega y Gasset (1959) expresses the thought that "they do not know what is happening to them and that is precisely what is happening to them . . ." (p. 119). There is both an absence of knowledge and an absence of thought about the perspective that drives us. Consequently, there is little understanding of the world view.

Perspective drives the way a person sees the world and his own personal world view. It drives everything that we do, and most of us follow the prevailing world view and adopt it as our perspective.

For several years after my return from Africa, I wallowed contentedly in middle class comfort. I was happily married, with a family, a secure career, and an economic well-being that gave me access to many worldly comforts. I believed that the world was becoming a better place through the application of technology, and I unthinkingly followed the prevailing world view. It was far easier to flow with the tide, accepting and implementing each educational fad as it moved through the educational system.

Each new strategy promised total success. There was little need to read or consider any research when you just had to sit and wait for the entertaining speakers to arrive in town with the next "solution." There is probably no one right answer to all problems, and yet we welcome the fads as they keep arriving. Each fad offered to solve all of our problems in a new way. I now believe that we need to take from the new, add to the best of the old, and not just throw everything out each time a new fad or strategy arrives.

Perspective Reexamined

Returning to university when I was the father of four children, two of whom had left home, marked a renewal of my journey to thoughtfulness. I made a determined commitment to a challenging and demanding program, but I was totally unprepared for the shock of my first summer back at university. I was challenged to examine my view of the world and consider my perspective of life. It was a great shock to realize what had been happening to me and the world in which I live. Alternative perspectives were a jolt, and I became aware that I truly did not know what was happening. What was new and challenging about the world views presented was that there *was* a world view, that there had been more than one world view historically, and that the world view had not changed for the better.

I now join Rifkin in questioning the idea that history is a record of progress and that the world is getting better with the passage of time (Rifkin, 1989, p. 21). I wonder whether the native peoples of North America were better off after the white man arrived. I wonder whether the people of Africa are better off since we forced our "civilization" on them. We feel good if we work only 40 hours a week and get three weeks of holiday a year. In Japan, the father often gets up before his children wake up and returns home after they have gone to sleep. This pattern is repeated six days each week.

Many people in "primitive" hunter-gatherer societies work for less than 20 hours a week and have months of time to pursue leisure activities. Increasingly we are becoming aware that the diet of hunter-gatherers or even subsistence farmers is nutritious and that they enjoy good health, while the diet of our western society is continually under suspicion as a cause of health problems. I remember old Mr. Mulonga who used to come to my door in Zambia to gather used tin cans and sell me eggs. He recycled the cans into drinking vessels in his village. He was a caring man, sometimes troubled about balancing his attentions among his three wives, but living a relatively stress free life. He spoke very few words of English, and I wonder now if he was not much better off than I was. Furthermore, their society was based on sharing and cooperation, both of which continue to be challenging and seemingly unattainable goals for our society (Rifkin, 1989, p. 25).

My perspective has changed, and after a period of some discomfort, I have felt a rise in integrity. Why did my perspective change? Why did I reexamine, reflect, and reconsider? The sudden realization and consequent refocus of myself fit with my belief that changes in the world sometimes can occur as a series of catastrophes rather than in a smooth and orderly manner (Velikovsky, 1950). However, science would have us believe that change is measured, gradual, organized, and calculated.

Man, by his nature, is an inquirer (Tinder, 1980). He is also by his nature thoughtful, that is to say, when man is left without the influences and pressures of our technological world, he is thoughtful. This can be observed in young children who, without any formal instruction, are naturally inquisitive, and allow themselves to become perplexed when considering the information they have received. It is a tragedy that many children lose this propensity to inquire and consider as they grow older. Through our thoughtfulness, we are able to unlock human potential (Gardner, 1990).

The technological world view would have us believe that life should be clean, precise, and exact. That is the high ground, but the issues of the high ground are unimportant (Schon, 1983). Life in the swamp is often messy, but "in the swamp lie the problems of greatest human concern" (Schon, 1983, p. 3).

Parents are increasingly becoming concerned about what is happening in schools and question if the schools really know what they are doing. To some extent, we are shielded from these parental pressures only by the thoughtlessness which prevails in our society. Yet we should remember that the problems of life and schooling are complex, usually multi-causal, and difficult to resolve.

I wonder how many of us as teachers care about either thoughtfulness or literacy and make either of them a priority in our classrooms? Perhaps it is fair to say that teachers do not realize that thoughtfulness is a problem. Most teachers are too busy dealing with the problems of teaching the prescribed curriculum and managing students with negative attitudes to schooling. Occasionally there are small pockets of concerned teachers, but, in spite of the efforts of the gallant few teachers, the prospects for well constructed thoughtful writing from the typical citizen of the future is unlikely. This is not because there has been a regression in thoughtfulness in schools or in our society, but rather that people in the western world never have been really thoughtful.

Writing is crucial because it requires you to think and organize your thoughts. Yet writing is viewed as children's work, something you have to do at school, but not something that is part of the adult world, the real world. For most citizens in our society, however, the question is, "why should we write?" What need does the typical citizen have for writing? Few people at work write sentences, much less paragraphs. A few words in the blank spaces on a form are usually sufficient. Even lawyers increasingly produce documents by selecting and fitting together blocks of text – almost as if they were playing with children's building blocks.

Reading fares only a little better than writing. Our society is increasingly peopled by the aliterate, those who have the knowledge and skills of literacy but choose not to use them. A survey conducted in the United States in 1969 indicated that 58% of American adults have never finished a book (Mikulecky, 1978). Increasingly there is less and less reading taking place outside of schools.

Education in the Future

We are walking down a path to a future world where literacy will be the domain of the few. This will mark a return to the medieval world where only the monks in their monasteries were literate. Will the professors in their ivory towers become the monks of the future? Will those practicing the skills of literacy be considered the elite, or just the unusual?

Can this be avoided? The back-to-the-basics and competency-based education movements only lead to minimal levels of literacy. Minimums too easily become maximums, and low standards are set for all. Standardized tests are neither fair nor valuable nor authentic. They perpetuate the focus on low standards. Society neither seems to understand what literacy is nor demand it. What can schools do about literacy? It is unlikely that schools will do anything about literacy because they do not recognize the prevailing world view. If you do not recognize the perspective that drives you, then it is difficult to tackle the problems you cannot see. If the society which creates the problem does not address the problem in a new way, then levels of functional literacy will continue to decline.

Is there no hope? Can we do anything? Each of us who sees and understands what is happening can only attempt to influence those we deal with. There can be preserved or developed small pockets of thoughtfulness where literacy is valued. We are left to swim upstream, as role models, struggling to keep our identity, and drowning in a morass of aliteracy.

The adults in school, including the teachers and administrators, should model thoughtfulness instead of demonstrating thoughtlessness. Example is one of the most powerful teachers. For this to happen, time may need to be allocated to the consideration and reflection of knowledge gained. There can be little thoughtfulness when learning consists of "facts in" and "facts out."

Thoughtfulness should be talked about and openly discussed as an educational objective. Awareness could develop into expectation.

Thoughtfulness is a disposition, which means that it is a bias or propensity to act in a certain way. Thoughtfulness requires perplexity, and can be self-imposed so that you seek out challenging questions, or it can be imposed by others. It is hoped that perplexity is imposed by teachers so that we "engage students so thoroughly in important questions that they learn to take pleasure in seeking important knowledge" (Wiggins, 1989, p. 49). Catastrophe, where the extremes of perplexity are reached, is thought-provoking as reality is reexamined with some urgency. We do not have much choice about the occurrence of catastrophes.

What matters most – what we teach, or what students learn? This question was provoked by reading Wiggins (1989), who asserts that "wisdom matters more than knowledge" (p. 58), and joins Mitchell in being concerned not just about acquiring knowledge, but also about our use of knowledge. Am I really on a journey through life trying to improve on the condition of mankind? Can I look a concerned or even an angry parent in the eye and profess that I am involved in education because I am concerned about children and enhancing their learning? Do I blindly follow societal trends and go along with what is popular – or do I examine my actions in the light of what I believe to be true? Should an increase in thoughtfulness, which is the work of the mind, be recognized as an important goal of schooling?

Garry McKinnon is in his eleventh year as Superintendent of Schools for the County of Wheatland, located forty kilometres east of Calgary, Alberta. In addition to his fourteen years of experience as a school system administrator (four as Deputy Superintendent for his present district), he has had ten years' experience in schools, as a junior-senior high school teacher, guidance counsellor, vice-principal, and principal. He has B.Ed. and B.Sc. degrees from the University of Saskatchewan, and a Graduate Diploma and an M.Ed. (Administration) degree from the University of Alberta. Garry received his Ed.D. degree from Brigham Young University in 1992. Garry and his wife, Doreen, live in Strathmore. They have a son in grade twelve and a daughter who is a third year education student.

4

Learning, Teaching, and Leading
– Some Observations Along the Way

Garry McKinnon

Describing my journey in search of a better understanding of learning, teaching, and leading has provided an opportunity to reflect on my experiences as a learner and educator. Frequently along the way, I have found that my paths as a learner and as an educator have converged, and I have developed a greater appreciation of the interrelationships between learning, teaching, and leading.

Gibboney (1987) refers to this interrelationship as he observes "leadership in education must be rooted in the fundamental enlightenment of thought – the intellectual and moral centre of education is learning and teaching" (p. 29). My journey is destined to lead to what Gibboney has described as the intellectual and moral centre of education, but I realize that it is a formidable undertaking, not unlike making a journey to the centre of the earth. We can easily be attracted by the appeal of educational bandwagons and rhetoric without even coming close to a glimpse of our destination. On the other hand, his reference to learning and teaching provides, for me, a focus for what I have to share.

I shall describe a journey, not to the centre of the earth, nor to the moral centre of education – it is a journey of reflections on my own personal observations and experiences as well as those of students, parents, and fellow educators. What I offer for learners, teachers, and leaders is food for thought, or what hopefully will be recognized later as "food for thoughtfulness." I begin with some reflections on my experiences as a learner.

During my early years as a learner in a small rural community in Saskatchewan, I benefitted from opportunities to develop close, personal relationships with my classmates and with my teachers. We shared ideas, challenged and supported each other, and we became a community of learners. Upon reflection on my grade one to twelve education, two teachers stand out as having had a special impact.

Mr. Brown, within the confines of one classroom, nurtured me through grades six, seven, and eight. He inspired me to think. He made learning meaningful through lively class discussions, projects, and special activities such as formal debates and presentations to parents and the members of the community. I believe Mr. Brown's key to success as a teacher was the ability to help his students develop confidence in themselves. His influence went beyond the classroom. He spent hours with us as our cub leader, boxing coach, and band master, always with an emphasis on confidence-building.

Mr. Josephson, our teacher in my senior high years, also helped me to develop confidence in myself as a learner. As well, he challenged his students to do more than what would normally be expected. For example, he went beyond the grade ten mathematics course by challenging us with university level calculus. I can recall my satisfaction in the first year of high school, in showing my older brother that I understood concepts he was struggling with in his university mathematics course. Mr. Josephson also taught us to think for ourselves. He constantly reminded us of the pressures of conformity which prevailed in our society. His challenge to us as students was "dare to be different." I have forgotten the calculus he taught us, but I have not forgotten the lesson of seeking out challenges and going beyond mediocrity.

As a confident high school graduate, I began my university education as a chemistry/mathematics major. To add some balance to my program, I elected to take a Canadian history course. I didn't realize at the time, as I do now, how fortunate I was to be in the class of Dr. Hilda Neatby. As a professor, she made history come alive, and she made learning meaningful. Her lectures were followed by a weekly seminar group which provided an opportunity to interact directly with her great mind. Dr. Neatby took time to make comments and raise questions on the papers which we wrote for her. I took special care in my writing and in the comments I made in class because I knew a great mind would be considering my thoughts. I was reminded of the significance of the impact she had on me as an educator when at a conference, Solway (1989) referred to Neatby, author of the book *So Little for the Mind* (1953), as one of the great Canadian educators. For her work as an educator, Dr. Neatby received the ultimate recognition, the Order of Canada.

I also took several graduate level courses from Dr. MacIntosh at the University of Alberta. He used the background experiences and knowledge of his students as a foundation for further learning and what he described as "making connections." From Dr. MacIntosh, I learned to connect my knowledge, experiences, and ideas as building blocks of personal meaning and what I have come to see as my "frame of reference" as an educator.

Over the past twenty-three years as a teacher, counsellor, school administrator and school system administrator, I have had the opportunity to refine my beliefs about learning and teaching and through my various roles, to test out these beliefs. I have been fortunate not only in having the opportunity to work directly with students, but also to be able to observe teachers and students in a variety of situations.

The Brigham Young University Experience

As I continued my journey as a learner, I expected the Brigham Young University doctoral program to focus primarily on such things as current theories of leadership, educational reform models, and the latest techniques for effective leadership. I was surprised, however, by the program outline given by the chairman and our key professor, Dr. Shute. Instead, Dr. Shute described the importance of perspective in determining how people think and what they do. It was his goal for us to become aware of our perspectives as educators, and to better understand the impact of perspective on our values and beliefs as they relate to learning and teaching.

Dr. Webb (1991), another Brigham Young professor, collaborates: "Teaching thoughtfully stems from a perspective – one's way of viewing, generally, teaching and learning – rather than from a programmed method. It's a kind of understanding or framework for understanding rather than a device or tool to be employed" (p. 1).

Their emphasis on what we have come to describe as "thoughtful" learning and teaching provided the impetus to reexamine some of the experiences I have had as a learner and a teacher.

Reflections as Learner

As I reflect on my experiences as a learner, I see common threads of meaning. These key teachers I have described have helped me to realize the importance of making learning meaningful, building on what has been learned, helping students make connections, and developing confidence. They modelled learning and collaborated as they built a community of learners. As well, I have found that these basic learning and teaching beliefs and practices are key elements of leadership. In fact, I am convinced that the essence of teaching is also the essence of leadership. These are guiding principles which I will take with me throughout my journey. So how do these principles relate to "thoughtfulness" and "perspective"? I offer further elaboration.

Thoughtful Learning and Teaching; Thoughtful Leadership

The conventional meaning of thoughtfulness involves caring about others. We could say that a thoughtful teacher is an individual who cares about students as individuals and cares enough to provide them with meaningful learning experiences, or what I would describe as opportunities for making connections and making personal sense of the world in which we live. Undoubtedly, the term is more complex. To attempt to define it or to list characteristics or conditions for thoughtful learning and teaching, I believe, would be inappropriate. When I reflect on my experiences as a learner and the special qualities of the teachers which I have described, I would say they have a disposition of thoughtfulness. What do I mean by disposition? Quite simply, I would describe it as a habit, a perspective, or a frame of reference which guides our thoughts and actions. Shute (1991), in describing the disposition of thoughtfulness, observes:

> The fostering of students' personal meaning is at the heart of thoughtful teaching and learning and the most important, yet most neglected aspect of schooling in America today. And the reason it is neglected is because personal meaning is not considered as being important under our present and modern frame of reference. (p. 16)

and he further observes:

> If inquiry is absent, personal meaning is absent. And, if personal meaning is absent, there is no learning. How does a teacher foster the kind of learning that I have been talking about? Actually, this can only be done by teachers who are learners, who learn by inquiry and who make personal sense of things – and all the while, allow children to observe them as they do so. It is manifestly impossible to be a "thoughtful" teacher and not model learning. (p. 18)

Interestingly, Shute refers to making personal meaning through inquiry, and he recognizes the importance for teachers of fostering inquiry and being models of learning.

Two Contrasting Learning and Teaching Perspectives

Dr. Shute has sharpened my awareness of the power of perspective which in turn has caused me, in my work with teachers in their classrooms, to be more inquiring and more reflective. I offer as illustration what could be described as representative of the prevailing learning and teaching perspective and a contrasting "thoughtful" perspective.

Typically and traditionally, the most common approach in evaluating a teacher has been to concentrate on standard indicators of teaching. Reference is made to the teacher's planning to ensure long range and unit plans are in place enabling the teacher to be fully prepared for what needs to be taught. The teacher's lesson plan is one source of information. Consideration is also given to how adequately the curriculum is being covered. The system of evaluation that the teacher has established is examined to determine if students are being evaluated regularly and if there are indicators that they are experiencing success. As well, provincial examination results and the scores on standardized tests are used as evidence of the effectiveness of the teacher.

In terms of the interaction between the teacher and the students, the emphasis is on classroom management. Determining whether the teacher demonstrates the use of effective disciplinary techniques and whether the students are conducting themselves in a responsible and orderly manner is paramount. As well, the effectiveness of the teacher is quantified by the percentage of time-on-task using an observation instrument.

An examination is made of the students' written work, with the major emphasis being on neatness and organization. In regard to the relationship between teacher and students, consideration is given to the degree of respect shown to the teacher.

On the other hand, one could approach a visit to a classroom from a different perspective. Rather than being concerned with the documentation available on the teacher's planning, the observer's emphasis would be on the meaningfulness of learning activities. The observer would look for indicators such as: types of questions students are asking, comments students make, and degree to which the teacher is functioning as a facilitator of learning as opposed to a dispenser of information.

Consideration would also be given to the relationship between the teacher and the students: Is there evidence of mutual respect, open communication, and a sense of collaboration in the learning process? Is the teacher modelling learning? Are students highly motivated and enthusiastically involved in learning activities? Is attention being given to determining whether or not there is a sense of freedom and a sense of purposefulness as opposed to regimentation and mindlessness?

In regard to the evaluation of students, one would ask: Are a variety of authentic assessment techniques and approaches being used? Does the teacher use evaluation feedback to organize learning activities based on individual student needs and learning styles?

In considering these two perspectives on teacher evaluation, the first would be described as a technological, results-based perspective. The second reflects a "thoughtful" frame of reference.

Solway (1990) describes the impact of the technological mindset or perspective on schools. For example, he explains how the focus on the mechanics of teaching has caused teachers to deal with the rules of grammar to such an extent that the real meaning of literature is lost. As well, he observes, learning has become mechanical, with an emphasis on input and output.

Mitchell (1984) is also very critical of education at all levels because of the technological perspective which prevails. He believes there is too much emphasis on workbooks and meaningless learning activities. He identifies the need to provide students with opportunities to make personal sense of the world, and to provide students with information and experiences which will become part of their knowledge base.

With these ideas in mind, I continue my journey as I consider the learning and teaching process from the perspective of students, teachers, and parents.

Each year, as part of the planning and goal setting process in our school system, a series of think tank sessions are held. The think tank sessions provide opportunities for groups of students, teachers, and parents to identify concerns, share ideas, and to reflect on the state of education. The collaborative views from the Think Tank Sessions are presented to the school system administrators and trustees at an annual planning workshop.

The Students' Point of View

I have been very impressed with the students' perceptiveness and their understanding of learning and teaching. Students indicated that they like to have hands-on activities and learning experiences which make what is being studied more relevant. They see value in experiments, projects, and activities such as field trips and student exchanges which take the learning beyond the classroom. Students believe that teachers should enjoy teaching. Teaching is an important role because teachers are seen as mentors and role models. Students feel teachers should work hard to challenge them and to help them learn. They appreciate teachers who make learning meaningful, and welcome innovative teaching approaches that go beyond what is in "the book." It is interesting that their descriptors of what is important to them relate closely to what I have described as the disposition of thoughtfulness.

The Teacher Perspective

A major problem for teachers, I believe, is that they do not find many opportunities to philosophize, to think about teaching practices, and to interact intellectually with other professionals. In addition to the annual teacher think tank session in our school system, we have formed the "Learning and Teaching Group" which meets regularly to share opinions, raise new ideas, and consider the meaning of learning and teaching in an informal setting. The time I have spent with this group of educators has proven to be a truly exciting experience, one that I would consider to be a key point along my journey to understanding learning, teaching, and leading.

So what are some of the thoughts of our teachers? They are concerned with the increasing expectations placed on schools and the overwhelming changes taking place in education. As well, dealing with students with behavioral problems and those with social/emotional problems is seen as a major source of frustration. Provincial examinations and standardized tests also intensify the pressure.

As well, teachers would like to have more input in the curriculum decisionmaking process. They believe curriculum expectations and the pressures of external examinations have caused educators to lose sight of some basic assumptions or beliefs in regard to learning and teaching which in the past have guided them in their work with their students. They feel that the first step in curriculum development should be to recognize that it is not possible to teach everything. Learning should be an active process rather than the passive receiving of facts.

Teachers are enthused about some changes which are taking place at the school, school system, and provincial level. These changes include the whole language philosophy, the process approach to teaching mathematics and science, and the inquiry approach in social studies.

I am excited about much of what our teachers are doing. I am convinced that in our school system we have a strong base on which to build.

The Parent Perspective

Through the Think Tank Sessions, parents had an opportunity to comment on their perceptions of the education of their children. Parents appreciate the efforts of teachers in fostering a positive self-image and in helping students develop confidence. They describe the importance of confidence-building and the human aspects of education as essential building blocks for learning.

Parents believe students will benefit from the opportunities of individualized learning experiences, provided teachers ensure the learning experiences are meaningful. They feel that the quality of education in the basics (whatever that may mean) is excellent. However, they believe there is too much emphasis on memorization and "book learning," and not enough opportunities for children to be challenged to learn through personal experience.

The parents indicated that they appreciate teachers who stimulate a love for learning among all students, show creativeness in teaching, and help students develop to their fullest, and they appreciate those teachers who work together with them to do what is best for their children.

At our most recent Think Tank session, the parents developed the following statement:

> In the world in which we live, information that is available to be learned is increasing extremely rapidly. It isn't possible to teach students everything that perhaps they should know. Although there is some information that should be basic for all students, there is a need to move away from all the emphasis on memorization of information and a heavy content orientation.
>
> To accomplish this goal, teaching will have to be significantly different from what it was a few years ago. Students need to learn how to access and use information. They need to be problem solvers and critical thinkers. Parents recognize that many teachers are making changes in what they are doing to foster the development of problem solving skills in their students. They realize teachers make the difference. Some are able to be more effective in this area than others but it is something that all teachers should be working on.
>
> The issues approach which is used in social studies and a focus on relating history to current events are examples of what is being done now to foster student thinking. As well, the changes in the teaching of math and science using hands-on experiences and the whole language approach in teaching language arts seem to have made learning more meaningful. (County of Wheatland, 1991)

I was impressed with the insight of the parents. Although they were unaware of what has been described as thoughtful learning and teaching, their views were most supportive of this framework.

A Closer Look at Learning and Teaching in the Classroom

With the thoughtful learning and teaching frame of reference in mind, I spent several months taking a closer look at the work of teachers and students in our schools; after all, that is where the action is. Representative of what impressed me are the thoughts of an elementary school principal:

> We need to provide opportunities for students to enhance their thinking skills. I don't think we can expect the same things from all students, but I think that the same road is open to them all and that we are there to facilitate and to motivate. We need to motivate them to do it. I believe the best way is by example, because students learn through the examples that the teachers set themselves in the classroom. If I show myself in the classroom to be the type of person who is constantly inquiring about things, that encourages the students to be like that as well. On the other hand, if I am a teacher who is content to deal with just what is in the book- "we have covered that, now let's go on to the next thing" – the students become content with that approach. Above all, teachers are role models. I guess the important question here though

is, role models of what? I think one of the most powerful things that I have seen in developing students is that teachers are using student-initiated activities. This helps to develop relevance and at the same time the students take ownership of what is happening. We tend to provide gifted kids with those types of activities, but I think it is something that we should be doing for every student in every subject. (McKinnon, 1991)

As well, I offer a description of a grade one classroom as representative of the classrooms I observed:

When I entered the classroom, the students were working on a math activity involving place value using base three as a number system. The students used strips of paper, lima beans, and little plastic cups to develop an understanding of the concept. As the students worked through the activities, the teacher asked them to think about what they had done and what it meant to them, as well as to look for patterns that had developed. With the input from the students, she made a summary of the observations on the chalkboard to demonstrate the patterns that could be identified. In so doing, she asked the students such questions as, "Can you predict what will happen next?" or "Do you see a pattern?" As the students worked through the system up to two hundred, she shared with them satisfaction in what they had accomplished.

I was impressed with the enthusiasm of the students, the success that they were experiencing, and the satisfaction that they got from understanding these concepts.

The approach that the teacher was using with manipulatives to experiment with different number systems in order to understand the basic fundamentals of the base ten system is relatively new in our school system. The teacher, who has taught grade one for over ten years, is enthusiastic about the use of the process approach in teaching mathematics. As well, over the past two years, she has adopted a whole language philosophy in teaching language arts, and has been experimenting with a process approach in teaching science and mathematics.

The physical arrangement of the classroom is conducive to a peer-teaching model which she uses extensively. There are tables for learning centers, and an excellent arrangement of resource materials and enrichment activities. The emphasis is on providing students with "hands-on" learning opportunities. She has created a very stimulating learning climate in her classroom through the use of a variety of charts and diagrams focusing on various concepts and samples of the students work.

In our discussions about her teaching, what impressed me most was the fact that she sees herself more as a learner than as a teacher.

Thoughtfulness – Sightings And Insights

It is interesting that what I have come to identify through my search for the disposition of thoughtfulness is closely related to what I have described as common threads of meaning in the experiences I have had as a learner. I share the following "sightings and insights."

Meaningfulness and Purposefulness

Unfortunately, in my search for the thoughtfulness disposition, I have observed situations in which mindlessness has prevailed. I have observed students filling in blanks in workbooks and being involved in other nonpurposeful activities. I have also seen students who were passive recipients of unrelated bits of information. Solway (1989) and Mitchell (1981) would say they are products of a technological mindset.

In my observations of classrooms in which students were involved in meaningful and purposeful learning activities, there was a sense of excitement and commitment on the part of the teacher and the students. The teachers made adjustments based on the students' individual needs, and the students were seen as active learners and partners in learning. As well, there were a variety of learning activities focusing on problem-solving and the fostering of inquiring minds. Meaningfulness, for me, is the fundamental indicator of thoughtful learning and teaching. As well, I believe the leadership challenge at all levels is one of developing a sense of purposefulness and meaningfully involving others.

Motivation

When working with teachers, frequent reference is made to the level of motivation of students. Sometimes, as well, a comment is made about the level of motivation of the teacher. The teacher is seen as being responsible for ensuring that the students are highly motivated. The level of motivation quite often is judged by measures such as time-on-task and student achievement. In my observations, teachers who have highly motivated students are mentors and models of learning. "We become more powerful as we nurture the power of those below us. One way to nurture those below us is by becoming a role model for how we want them to function" (Block, 1987, p. 64).

DePree (1989) elaborates further: "The signs of outstanding leadership appear primarily among the followers. Are the followers reaching their potential? Are they learning, serving?" (p. 20).

Teachers who are mentors of learning do not seem to be concerned with motivation because it occurs naturally when thoughtfulness prevails. I believe leaders at all levels must first and foremost be learners and motivate others by mentoring learning.

Confidence-Building

I have found confidence-building to be very important in the learning and teaching process. I have seen students who resist active involvement in learning because they do not believe they are capable of learning. It appears they do not have confidence in themselves. The teacher, as leader, needs to be a confidence-builder by providing opportunities for students to experience success and to build on their success. A student has to have the confidence base in order to be a risk-taker and a learner.

Gardner (1990) reaffirms the importance of a leader as a confidence builder. He sees leaders as not only being confident, but also as having a capacity to communicate confidence. Thus it is important for teachers and other leaders to have a positive orientation, and to have confidence in themselves and those they lead.

Perceptiveness

In working with teachers who are experiencing difficulty with students, I have found that often the problem is one of not having a "good reading of the situation." Teachers, as leaders, must be perceptive. Teachers/leaders are what I describe as "finely tuned" in terms of their perceptiveness. Bennis (1990) describes perceptiveness as the "factor x of leadership" and he observes that "a leader knows what we want and what we need before we do and expresses these unspoken dreams for us in everything that he or she says or does" (p. 159).

The importance of perceptiveness is also supported by those writing about a new style of leadership based on intuition. Desjardins and OsmanBrown (1991) describe our intuitiveness and how it can lead to a new way of formulating questions and seeking answers (getting a good reading of the situation) through reflecting on one's own voice and intuitive wisdom.

Establishing Positive Relationships

Gardner (1990) describes a universal fundamental component of leadership – a leader cannot lead without having followers. Teachers as leaders in their classrooms may have the obedience of their students but the influence will be shallow unless there is a relationship which is based on trust. I find myself frequently describing the process of establishing relationships with students as "building bridges." It is essential for the teacher to build a bridge of trust and mutual respect with each student. The bridge provides the structure for two-way interaction. Some teachers, in considering the relationship they have with their students, describe what in many ways can be seen as a loving relationship in which the teacher contemplates the question, "What is the loving thing to do in this situation?"

Bennis and Nanus (1985) observe that leadership is essentially a human business, and that leaders showing a positive regard for others describe it as being a pivotal factor in their capacity to lead. As well, the feasibility of a leader serving his constituents as a servant leader is dependent on a sense of togetherness and a common focus (Greenleaf, 1977).

Communication

Establishing open communication, I believe, is a very important challenge for teachers and leaders. There are many barriers to communication which must be overcome. I have found in those classrooms where communication appears to be top down, something is lacking. Conversely, where there is open, direct communication and a two-way sharing of ideas and information, there is much to behold. Bennis and Nanus (1985), comment: "There are a lot of intoxicating visions and a lot of noble interactions. Many people have rich and deeply textured agendas but, without communication, nothing will be realized" (p. 33). Peters and Waterman (1982) describe how leaders identify respect for people in face-to-face communication as being fundamental.

Putting It All Together

Meaningfulness and purposefulness, confidence-building, perceptiveness, establishing positive relationships, and communication, I believe, all relate to what Brown (1987) has described as "providing the setting and the incentives for doing thoughtfully and humanely the work of the mind" (p. 49). I conclude that they are descriptors of the disposition of thoughtfulness.

The Skills Question

What I have described up to this point is a frame of reference or what I have referred to as a disposition. Is there a place for teaching skills? I have come to look at the skills issue in terms of the art and science of teaching. The science of teaching involves techniques and skills which the teacher can use in organizing learning activities in the classroom. Unfortunately, the prevailing technological frame of reference is very much concerned only with the science of teaching. On the other hand, the thoughtfulness frame of reference, I believe, accentuates the art of teaching. The challenge for teachers and leaders, I conclude, is to focus on the art as well as the science of learning, teaching, and leading.

Learning and Teaching Paradigms and the Change Process

Along this journey, I have come to believe that there is a need for significant change in our schools which can only be achieved through what Fullan (1991) describes as "fostering a new way of thinking and doing" (p. 84). If we are going to bring about change, we have to move from the prevailing teaching paradigm to the thoughtful learning and teaching paradigm. To illustrate, I offer the following description of the two paradigms.

The Prevailing Teaching and Learning Paradigm:

1. There are primarily teacher-directed learning activities.

2. The child is a passive receiver of information who is dependent on the teacher.

3. Instruction is generally for the whole group.

4. Students work independently at their desks.

5. The material dealt with is determined by external curriculum and examinations.

6. Subjects are taught separately.

7. Students are frequently involved in mindless activities including the use of workbooks and some computer programs.

8. Single correct answers are sought out.

9. The teacher is seen as the sole arbitrator of what is correct.

10. Assessment is of what a child already knows and is for classification and reporting purposes.

11. The child is the recipient of the teacher's knowledge.

12. Answers (as opposed to questions) are valued.

The Thoughtful Learning and Teaching Paradigm:

On the other end of the continuum, there is a paradigm of "thoughtful" learning and teaching:

1. Where appropriate, teachers make adjustments based on student individual needs.

2. The child is an active learner.

3. The child is a partner in learning.

4. Instruction is provided in whole groups, small groups, and individually.

5. The children's capacity to learn is extended.

6. Materials used and learning experiences are based on the child's capacity to learn (e.g. continuous progress).

7. The subjects are integrated.

8. There is a variety of learning resources including quality literature.

9. The emphasis is on problem solving and thinking.

10. Rather than single answers, alternate solutions are generated.

11. Children are seen as theory-builders and negotiators.

12. Assessment focuses on how a child learns and what a child can do.

13. Assessment is on-going for purposes of instructional decision making.

14. The students are collaborators in their own learning.

15. Questions are valued.

So how do we bring about this change or paradigm shift? Smith (1986), whose views have recently impacted my thinking, says that we have to do away with the belief that experts outside the classroom can make better decisions about helping students learn than the teachers who actually see and talk with the students. Control for learning has to return to the teachers. In describing how this is to be done, he comments: "We need to shift the focus of learning from simply teaching students to have the right answer to teaching them the process by which educated people pursue the right answers" (p. 139).

He identifies two essential characteristics of all good teachers: "They are interested in what they teach and they enjoy working with learners – indeed, they are learners themselves" (p. 173). In describing how teachers need to deal with the influences of a programmed learning mindset, Smith says "teachers need to be transformed from being classroom managers to becoming effective leaders" (p. 240). How do teachers do this? Smith offers: "Once again, the best way to educate is through demonstration. If there is one thing that persuades teachers and administrators, it is success" (p. 241).

I certainly agree with Smith's analysis that teachers must change themselves before they can change others. I realize that it is not an easy process, but I am very excited about the potential to bring about significant change in our schools and I know it can be done. I have seen what teachers can do, individually and collectively, when they are given an opportunity to think about learning and teaching, to discuss concerns and share ideas, to develop shared meaning and take ownership for change, and to work collaboratively with their fellow teachers and their students.

Concluding Comments

As I reflect on my journey in search of an understanding of learning, teaching, and leading, I have concluded that there are fundamental elements which have always existed, but have been lost to a significant degree because of the overwhelming technological mindset which prevails. I believe a shift in perspective toward a thoughtfulness paradigm provides the key to bringing about significant change in education. As well, I have come to realize that the thoughtfulness paradigm is also a fundamental source of understanding a new approach to leadership, which is also required to foster change in our schools.

Working with the Brigham Young University Alberta Group of Ten, in reflecting on our personal and collective learning and teaching journeys, has been both interesting and demanding. This experience as a community of learners has been tremendously stimulating. In sharing ideas and drafts with the group, I have struggled with this description of my personal journey. I made the mistake of telling my colleagues about my walk each evening with my dog, Gizmo, and my dictaphone. As I walked, I used my dictaphone to record my thoughts and ideas. Among the comments from the group were, "I bet Gizmo is the most thoughtful dog around," and, "What a way to walk the talk." I have seen signs that Gizmo has been influenced by daily exposure to my ideas on thoughtful teaching and leading. She seems to wag her tail more thoughtfully and she seems to be trying harder to make meaning of the world around her, but I can't be sure. I am equally uncertain about the impact on those who read this description of my personal journey. It is my hope that it will stimulate thought and cause the reader to reflect, and that it will foster a search for personal meaning and understanding. Have I come to what Gibboney described as the moral centre of education? Definitely not, but I believe I am on the right track. It has been and it will continue to be an interesting journey.

The challenge for educational leaders is to help teachers assume a leadership perspective as well as a learning and teaching perspective, and to help leaders assume a learning and teaching perspective as well as a leadership perspective. I recognize that the learning and teaching perspective and the leadership perspective are closely related. The thoughtful learning and teaching and thoughtful leadership paradigm offers a significant opportunity for all educators. Join me as we walk the thoughtful talk, as the journey toward a better understanding of learning, teaching, and leading continues.

Jean Hoeft was an elementary school teacher before becoming a Language Arts Specialist for the Calgary Board of Education. She has studied with Margaret Meek and James Britton at the University of London, England, and is also a graduate of the University of Saskatchewan and the University of Calgary. Last year she co-authored the Teachers' Resource Manual to accompany the new Language and Learning Program of Studies for Alberta Education. She has devoted considerable effort to help teachers become reflective learners in their own classrooms and is interested in the wide range of children's language development, especially in their writing and the role of language in learning.

5

Teacher Stories:
Thoughtful Voices from the Classroom

Jean Hoeft

Our elementary school was in a small town in Saskatchewan. We didn't have a library in the town or the school. About three times a year, the school unit would send us a box of about twenty books, both fact and fiction. They were kept on two shelves at the back of the classroom. I remember being so excited about being able to take these books home to read. Sometimes my mom and I read the books together. However, the best times were when my friend Clara and I read the same book. We had great discussions walking to and from school debating the merits of what we had read. We played house and pretended to be the characters. Sometimes we acted out a whole story and sometimes we changed the endings. We made paper dolls and set up scenes for playing out the stories. Oh, how we loved those books! We read every book that arrived in those boxes. I remember a science book we both read about butterflies. We pretended we were scientists looking for cocoons and made nets to capture butterflies. I don't recall ever catching one, but I do remember a wonderful kite we made and decorated with a beautiful, colorful butterfly. To this day, I can still remember all sorts of facts about the life of a butterfly.

Kay Anderson

Kay Anderson, a teacher and colleague, wrote this brief reflective story at my prompting. I had asked a group of teachers who had been engaged in a project to write about an incident in their lives or the lives of their students that illustrated thoughtfulness. As a group, we had spent a great deal of time talking about what happens when you engage students in thoughtful learning – making meaning for themselves as well as others.

Like Kay, I remember growing up in a small town in Saskatchewan. I also remember that small box of books that arrived monthly and our excitement at exploring its contents – the contents that allowed me to choose what I wanted to learn about. And now once again I find myself with boxes full of books –

Gibboney, Smith, Sizer, Goodlad, Dillon, Barth, Schön, Langer, Solway, and many, many more.

A unique doctoral program at Brigham Young University afforded me the opportunity to explore new theories and knowledge and relate them to my work with teachers. This program allowed me to become a researcher, an observer, a questioner, a learner, and a more thoughtful educator – a researcher in the sense of looking and looking again at what we do as teachers and learners, an observer in the sense of causing me to question many of my beliefs and assumptions about learning, a questioner in the sense that problems can become questions to be investigated and occasions for learning, and a learner in the sense of doing what one believes about teaching and learning. This program has helped me become a more thoughtful educator.

Historically, teachers and teacher educators could regard their task as being straightforward. There was a body of knowledge, specific skills and content to be transmitted. Despite some attempts to change pedagogical practice, the fundamental transmission model used in schools has remained relatively unchanged over this century. Recent perceptions of a crisis in education have given rise to many proposed solutions. Most of these solutions have not challenged the transition model. Our inability to make change in this model lies in the philosophy and science of the West. Modern science and technology are responsible in large measure for the prevailing technological mindset. Gibboney (1991) argues:

> Fundamental reform in the schools is blocked by a habit of mind, the tendency to view education from the narrow perspective of the technological mindset. This mindset drives our inability to move away from this "transmission model of teaching" and stops us from moving into new ways of teaching. Fundamental reform is reform that is intellectual and democratic. (p. 683)

If teaching and learning are to be both intellectual and democratic, then we must change teaching from a transmission model to a democratic model where students are allowed to wrestle with new ideas and create meaning for themselves. In this model of teaching, the teacher is also a learner and the student is also a teacher.

Brown (1988) defines clearly and simply what he means by literacy and thoughtfulness. He wants learners both young and old to be involved in inquiry, discovery, learning, collaborative problem solving and critical thinking. If you want people to think, then ask them hard questions and give them the time and resources to wrestle with the answers. He also observes that good schools are symbolically rich places, where interesting conversations are taking place. Conversations that occur in the form of teacher stories often reflect on teaching. These stories often lead to the examination of our beliefs and assumptions about thoughtful learning. Brown also believes that if you want to change individuals, you usually have to make them conscious of things that are right in front of them. You have to help them learn how to listen to themselves, how to recognize what they are saying, how to discover their underlying beliefs and assumptions. Conversations in the form of stories help teachers examine their practice.

What I want to do is to examine teacher stories that illustrate thoughtfulness. The word "story" can be traced to the Greek word *eidenai*, which means "to know." As a learner, I look to teachers' stories to help me understand and to give meaning to my own understanding. These teacher stories are rich in the language of exploration and reflect their attempts to make meaning for themselves as well as for their colleagues. Although Kay knew her story held an important lesson for her and for her teaching, she had difficulty at first realizing how writing her story could help her give meaning to thoughtfulness. Schön (1983) asks:

> What is the kind of knowing in which competent practitioners engage? . . . practitioners do reflect on their knowing-in-practices. They think back on a project they have undertaken, a situation they have lived through, and they explore the understanding they have brought to their handling of the case. (p. 61)

For us as teachers, it is often difficult to realize the importance of our stories and how they assist us in formulating our beliefs about learning. Our stories illustrate our experiences as learners. These experiences are closest to us, they are first hand and drive much of what we believe to be true about teaching and learning. As we worked together in study groups, we shared each other's writings and thoughts. The writing helped each of us formulate thoughts and made our thoughts public to the rest of the group. Schön goes on to emphasize the importance of sharing one's thoughts with others ". . . the teacher's isolation in her classroom works against reflection-in-action. She needs to communicate her private puzzles and insights, to test them against the views of her peers" (p. 333). By bringing my knowing and doing together, and by creating groups of teachers who were interested in learning with me, I was able to move towards becoming thoughtful. The study group allowed me the opportunity to expand my idea of research, which is not primarily a process of proving something, but rather a process of discovery and learning. This view of research proved to be very liberating and allowed teachers to take seriously the ordinary "stories" of their teaching lives.

Educators have often asked whether it is possible to teach and do research at the same time. This question reflects the separation we often feel between knowing and doing, and the division within our educational systems between those who "know" and those who "do." Smith (1988) talking about collaboration between educators states:

Learning itself has to be demonstrated. Many of the more general abilities that we strive to develop – like inquiry, questioning, problem solving, inference, critical thinking and collaboration itself – can only be demonstrated by experienced practitioners interacting with each other. (p. 76)

Voices coming from the classroom and from the teacher education community have begun to look afresh at the process of learning and teaching. They have begun to raise important questions about the "hows" and "whys" of education. These voices argue that the fundamental metaphors and theories in education must be re-examined. These are the voices of a more intellectual and democratic system.

Last year, I worked with three groups of teachers brought together to research an area of their own interest: a small group who used writing to reflect on how their students learn through language and the fine arts; a second group who focused on making their classrooms more meaningful for students by creating communities of learners; and last, a group who used their own personal journals to reflect on their practice. A journey of exploration runs through each story, validating the many different models of learning that are beginning to emerge in classrooms today.

In each group, the process involved writing their stories. Through their writing and through dialogue with their peers, the participants uncovered their beliefs. This provided a foundation for constructing meaning and making connections. Classroom inquiry can create a much bigger change in thinking and working in schools than we might expect. Teachers who cast themselves as learners redefine their roles in the classroom; they are part of classrooms that are "thoughtful communities." It is through my work with these thoughtful communities that I am able to confirm my own learning. It is through their journeys that I continue to understand my own thinking. Their journeys become my journey.

My journey is about change, not change in the abstract, but change that grows out of more thoughtful attitudes and assumptions about learning and teaching. It is about how I have changed and how this change has affected the way I work with teachers. My choice of strategies in different situations is determined by many factors: my assumptions about what teaching means, what I sense might be useful for the group, and my awareness of my own learning. I know that I am aware of some of the beliefs guiding my decisions, and I know that my beliefs are evolving because of my own personal experiences. My current thinking about teaching is the result of my journey. It is part of the formal study I have done and also the learning I am engaged in now – my ongoing conversations with my professors, classmates, colleagues and other teachers.

I began with Kay's story. Kay had been part of a special project that integrated the Fine Arts and Language Learning. Her writing was her way of making meaning for herself. Kay writes:

> My attitude began to change as these discussions progressed and plans for implementing the program continued. I was becoming convinced that not only would art enrich language, but the language would enrich art and learning for students would become more meaningful. Over the past two years I have come to understand that if you want to change individuals, you usually have to make them conscious of things that are not obvious to them. If you are able to help them learn how to listen to themselves through their writing, how to recognize contradictions, and patterns of expression that reveal underlying assumptions and beliefs.

Lynn, another member of this project, reflects on how learning changed for one of her students. She writes:

> Ernest read haltingly, his speech punctuated by a series of nervous giggles. As was customary after the reading, the children asked questions. It was in the answering of the questions that Ernest's presentation came alive because of his detailed and lively explanation of his drawings. Ernest did not relinquish his seat on the stool until the bell rang to end the day, fifteen minutes after he had sat down. Even as the children streamed from the room, the discussion continued. Little did I know then that Ernest and I were about to embark on a journey, an adventure in learning that would change us both.

She goes on to write about what happened to Ernest when he was allowed to choose his own topic for writing:

> Ernest was becoming actively involved in his learning. I watched as his learning was motivated by a desire to create, a desire to express himself through art. The lessons that Ernest taught me were many. Perhaps the most valuable was his helping me to understand the link between the process of creating a piece of art and the process of creating a piece of writing. Each is a process of constructing meaning for oneself and for others. Ernest taught me to accept the stories of the children in my class in whatever form they emerged.

Lynn's story illustrates how one young learner's explorations of the world through drawing and writing helped him to solve the problem of transferring the world of images to that of language. Through this story we also begin to see how teachers can influence different ways of developing thoughtfulness. Eisner (1981) puts forward the following thesis: "It is that the arts are cognitive activities, guided by human intelligence, that make unique forms of meaning possible" (p. 48). One of the basic problems we have in schools today is defining how knowledge is acquired and organized and how effective learning takes place. This teacher is beginning to articulate her stance about what she sees as knowledge. Lynn's view of knowledge shapes the way she organizes her classroom to allow for real learning to occur for her students.

Good teachers have always known how to make students think about and apply their knowledge. Good schools are language rich places, where vivid and interesting stories are being told. Adults are visibly engaged in inquiry, discovery, and learning. When teachers have the opportunity to write and reflect on their practice, they develop sound assumptions and beliefs about teaching and learning. It is critical to afford teachers these opportunities to develop their image of a thoughtful classroom.

The next story demonstrates opportunities for students to learn to read and write through an approach known as Readers' Workshop. Readers' Workshop is a way to promote thoughtfulness and represents a new approach developed by many teachers. Brown (1988) points out that several things suggest that thoughtfulness requires a different approach. A literacy of thoughtfulness is primarily a process of making meaning (not just receiving it) and negotiating it with others (not just thinking alone.) Readers' Workshop, first of all, is about making meaning for oneself and secondly, the broadening and consolidating of meaning through discussion with peers.

Graves (1990) says that when children share their reading of wonderful books, they encounter many minds: the teacher's, other children's, the author's and their own. Each provides space for the thinking of others. Readers' Workshop promotes authentic meaningful interaction allowing students to explore aesthetic qualities of text. This type of exploration seldom occurs when teachers guide students through activities looking for text-bound answers to teacher-generated questions. In most classrooms we find teachers talking about reading but not actually reading, talking about writing but not actually writing. Everything we do in the classroom is founded on a set of assumptions about teaching and learning, about knowledge, and about what counts as legitimate reading and writing. In Readers' Workshop, teachers believe you learn to read by reading and you learn to write by writing.

Pat and Jill write about Readers' Workshop. Pat begins by focusing on what real readers do when they read. She writes:

> First of all they make their own choices about what they will read. Then they spend a lot of time reading. Real readers love to "gossip" about what they have read, and make recommendations about good books to others. Readers' Workshop is simply a vehicle for allowing students the opportunity to do all these things. It is one way teachers and students can build a community of readers in which everyone is a reader.

Jill illustrates the processes involved in a workshop approach:

In Readers' Workshops students may use language as a "tool" to make meaning – to question, to compose, and to comprehend. While they often do this for themselves, just as often they make meaning to share with others. Learners may work alone, or they may gain from talk, reading and writing with others. They know that there is regular, daily, or predictable time to go about this reading, writing, and talking.

For some time the United States and Canada have been preoccupied with student improvement in both reading and writing. National reports speak of student failure and slipping test scores. For most people, being literate means being able to read, and the most significant aspects of reading are educational ones. It is in school that the standards of success are set. Readers' Workshop returns reading to a more natural endeavor by allowing readers to bring their own context to the meaning of the text. Readers recreate experiences, extend them, think about them, and even resist them. Through reading, we learn to make meaning. They go on to write about the importance of student response:

> After completing the assigned reading for the day, students respond to what they have read in response journals. The students may quote powerful or meaningful passages from the book, predict what might happen next, remark on similarities between the text and their own life, or pose questions about parts of the text that do not make sense to them.

Brown (1987) states, "Thoughtfulness requires close reading and disciplined debate about what has been read. It requires substantial writing" (p. 51). It is often beneficial to combine group discussion or debate with response journals. Questions, answers, and a change in perspective may result from further reading and in-depth discussion. Jill goes on to say:

> Students are empowered to use and share their own voices when teachers cease dominating the talk and allow students to learn collaboratively, to write in journals, to form book clubs and literature discussion groups, in other words to use all the ways we have of joining a social group. Today we know a great deal about the social nature of learning.

How does the act of writing help students think and learn? Simply stated, people cannot write unless they are thinking. Thinking propels the pen forward in a meaningful way. And it is the thinking and recording in a meaningful way that helps us to structure knowledge. With writing, there is a record of thinking for both the learners and teachers to see. Through the use of journals, both the student and teacher can examine the mind at work. Pat shares her thoughts:

> The journal is the key to what the student is thinking: how they are able to analyze and synthesize information; how they think critically, solve problems and use metacognition as a process for reflecting on their own learning. Portfolios are kept throughout the workshops and contain many artifacts of students work as they respond to the text in many formats.

Wolf (1989) states "when students maintain portfolios of their work, they learn to assess their own progress as learners, and teachers gain new views of their accomplishments on teaching" (p. 35). He goes on to say that through portfolios it is possible to access the thinking process in two ways. Portfolios provide information to teachers and school systems, and they also provide models for personal responsibility in questioning and reflecting on the students' own work. They capture growth over time so that students can become more informed and thoughtful assessors of their own histories as learners. Jill writes:

> Readers' Workshop is based on current research and sound teaching prac-
> tices. This approach allows students to read literature, to respond to the text,
> to use language for learning through discussion and written responses, to
> compare their interpretations of text with the thoughts of others, to develop
> portfolios of their work as evidence of their growth, and to become active
> participants in their evaluation.

We need to renovate education as carefully as we remodel our homes. After all, we have to live there. First, we must realize that we need a different effect. We then visualize exactly how we want the remodelled structure to look, check out the foundation, put up a sturdy framework, and finally, step back to view and evaluate the results of our labor. Readers' Workshop is shaped around these steps for renovation. We know that reading and writing to learn is an approach that will give classrooms a new look and will help students to learn better. We know that a workshop approach provides a sturdy framework of support, and we know that through writing real learning can be examined. Brown (1988) describes problems existing with traditional approaches:

> We already know that almost no intensive reading takes place, no extensive
> writing, and no classroom discussion or debate. There is simply no time for
> such things. Schooling places heavy emphasis on drill, memorization, recita-
> tion, seat work and teacher talk. (p. 4)

If we want to promote thoughtfulness in our classrooms, then perhaps Readers' Workshop is a viable alternative.

There is a preface to the last story, an important history that precedes formation of the group and in many ways contributed to its success. I first met these five teachers through my work and we shared the common experience of writing an informational pamphlet. During the writing of the pamphlet, these teachers were recognized as successful practitioners, were given a sense of belonging to a community of learners and began to develop an awareness of their own knowledge. On completion and publication of the pamphlet, these teachers decided to form a study group which would enable them to continue to learn and develop as teacher researchers.

Through this study group, I increased my understanding of how teachers can be researchers of their own practice. Through their writing, I learned that teachers need encouragement and confirmation as they find their own purposes and directions for their understandings. I also discovered that teachers feel tentative about sharing their ideas. I began to understand how I could serve as a mentor. My role was to ponder, wonder, and imagine with them as they tried to find meaning and focus their thoughts. Throughout the development of the pamphlet, I had beliefs and values that drive my perspective on how we learn in a community of learners. The formation of this study group gave me the opportunity to act on my beliefs and formulate how I might work with groups as they support one another in developing thoughtfulness. Wiggins (1987) confirms, "Thoughtfulness is a disposition – developed when one is regularly confronted with genuine intellectual problems that demand thought" (p. 74).

The story did not end when the pamphlet was completed, but really began when these teachers decided to meet on a regular basis and keep reflective journals. At first we discussed how individuals might find their own purposes for reflecting on practice. We spoke of looking at practice and engaging in thoughtfulness in order to improve teaching and thus real learning for students. Throughout this story, the importance of writing as a tool for thoughtfulness emerged. Traditionally in schools, writing has been regarded as a mode of expression chiefly used to indicate what has been learned. Even today, writing largely records knowledge, and there is very little evidence to indicate that students use writing as a learning process. By using journals, these teachers attempted to broaden their use of writing for learning and thus seek the same for their students. Wiggins states, "Thoughtful understanding cannot be taught insofar as that means handing out information. It must be constructed by the thinker" (p. 72). It is through writing that we are able to begin to think, reflect and ponder what we already know and what we want to know. Talk and learning allows learners to explore new understandings, to organize and give shape to their thought. Language makes connections between what we already know and what we want to know. Language is a tool for trying to understand the perceptions and experiences of the world we live in.

As each individual's purpose for writing unfolds, the style and structure of each journal evolves very differently. The journals change over time as focus and direction emerge and as individuals learn and grow. Questions emerge and shape ideas. The following entry shows how her journal allows this teacher the opportunity to reconstruct past experiences:

> Journals give me time to reflect on my learning – time to find threads – to go back and reflect again – to go back knowing more and to read my reflections again. I see things that I didn't see then . . . I realize that it takes time to come to know. My discoveries come from working on a question over time.

Whenever teachers engage in this type of dialogue, they reflect on their personal ways of being thoughtful in their classrooms. Wiggins (1987) supports this notion: "A thoughtful person has developed the habits of a scholar, not just the ability to mouth a scholar's results on cue" (p. 74). Another teacher talks about her work:

> Observation is key. Through daily observations, I make connections. They come from my purpose and my intentions. Each new observation is grounded in what went before.

Through her attempt to reflect on her observations, she begins to realize that her observation and reflections will continue to inform her practice.

As the year progressed, each journal was shared with all members of the group. We wrote responses to the journal entries. As a result of engaging in this form of thoughtfulness, new questions continued to form and reform. This is illustrated when Mary reflects on the importance of a colleague's response:

> As I reread my journal, I appreciate just how much support I am getting. I think it's the nature of the questions that arise through this kind of journal dialogue. Many of the questions cause new insights for me.

Wiggins (1987) explains what it is like to engage in thoughtful dialogue with oneself and others:

> Thoughtful understanding cannot be "taught." It must be constructed by the thinker. The development of thoughtfulness depends on the active, inquiring role played by the learner when putting ideas together to form personally meaningful versions of an important idea" (p. 72).

Susan reflects on the importance of receiving response from a number of colleagues:

> I look forward to spending more time reading and rereading what people have to say in my journal. The response is so valuable. I get a clearer picture of where I have come from and where I am going in my thinking.

She is right. Reading, reacting to, and relating the various responses is very important. I believe that this experience contributes to her ability to be thoughtful – an authentic situation that allows for her knowledge to be constructed. Through sharing with others in a trusting community, our thinking surfaces and our thoughts emerge. The group enhances my understanding and is helping me to grow. There are no identified models to follow, and I am firm in my belief that the sharing of our own stories is the key. Mary writes:

> Through my journal, I think I am looking at issues of education with greater enthusiasm. I think I will read all of my journal and mark the statements which really hit me; try to draw conclusions.

Teachers who decide to engage in this type of research must be recognized as thoughtful practitioners. Leaders of such communities must be open to different ways of thinking and feeling. They must be careful not to try to control the development of "thoughtfulness." They must be wary of silencing teachers' research voices. They must be prepared to involve themselves in knowing and caring for the teachers with whom they work, recognizing that through collaboration, thoughtfulness will occur.

As each story unfolded, it became a record of personal and professional growth through the establishment of thoughtful communities. As we came to value our own personal knowledge, we became reflective practitioners and researchers. As we came to value the knowledge and experience of our colleagues, a trusting, caring community developed that nurtured the growth of its individual members. Thoughtfulness comes from collaboration and reflection.

The study groups were central to each person's story. They provided the vehicle for learning and a place for thinking to take place. The groups provided the framework for developing communities of learners – an authentic audience for our stories. They also provided me with the insights into the particular skills required by leaders to work with constituents who are reflective practitioners. Smith (1986) hypothesizes that schools should be learning emporia, places where people congregate to learn, and no one should be there who does not want to participate in learning – whether the role is to be a student, a teacher, or an administrator.

We neither glossed over our differences nor ignored our sameness, and the integrity of each individual was preserved. We gained the courage to ask questions, explore, and challenge the assumptions underlying our practice. Our stories allowed us to share our beliefs and helped us make meaning for ourselves and others. We became more thoughtful.

As a writer, I tell stories about myself and about my colleagues so that I might better understand. This story is far from finished; in a sense, it is just beginning.

Irene Russell Naested was born in Beausejour, Manitoba. She received her B.Ed. degree and a M.A. in art education at the University of Calgary. Her teaching career has included elementary, junior and senior high school regular as well as special needs students, as well as college and university level. Irene has a strong belief in the fine arts in the education of children. She has written curriculum and articles based on these beliefs, and has lectured nationally and internationally. She lives in Calgary with her husband, Jesper, and their son, Thomas. She received her Ed.D. degree from Brigham Young University in 1992.

Transmission

- Certainty principle

Technological paradigm
        - thinking machine

standardized tests

registry of mind
    (filling of facts)
less time
desk sitting, listening reading

School

Multi-Sensory perceptive Modes

6

Toward the Forgotten Thoughtfulness

Irene Naested

When I was a child,

I played as a child.

When I became a student,

I was encouraged to put away my childish ways,

And decipher meaning from the world through word and number.

When I became a teacher,

I rediscovered the values of play,

And other ways to experience and learn.

Naested, 1991

Thoughtfulness Forgotten

The environment experienced by humans is both natural and man-made, filled with images, sounds, smells, movement, temperatures, animal and plant, and human life forms. To be a thoughtful learner one must develop the means for information gathering from many sources in order to consider all things. I have a strong belief that thoughtfulness prevails in environments where perceptive multi-sensory modes of information gathering, expression, and communication are promoted, encouraged, and where they become part of the cultural norms of the group and the individuals within the group. Words alone cannot completely help humans to understand the personal and cultural nature of thoughts and feelings even when all the words are commonly known.

North America has developed a culture with a technological mindset, where word and number are the primary ways humans perceive, express, and communicate. How has this affected our children, schools, and our western culture? I discuss this question by reflecting on a philosophy of how we learn as infants. All cultures naturally educate their infants to develop all their senses in order to learn and understand the world. Learning and communicating should use all of the senses. Humans have been blessed with five senses in order to learn, and a body, voice, and ability to make sounds and images in order to communicate. Why has this changed? How has this been forgotten?

The story of the student and the teacher are excerpts from my personal experiences. The classroom vignette relates thoughtful learning and teaching achieved by calling on the multi-senses. From this perspective, I discuss what I consider to be the forgotten thoughtfulness, that is, the thoughtfulness developed through perceptive information gathering, input, and communication.

The Infant

An unborn infant senses light, hears sounds from within the womb, and the sounds from the outside world. The unborn infant feels movement from its mother and her world, and moves about in the womb's predetermined space, touching with feet, hands, and body, somewhat confined, but definitely investigating the environment. The infant hears the rhythm of the mother's heart beat, sounds and songs she is singing and playing.

When the child is born into a culture, nurturing adults share their world with the infant through sound, images, movement, and words. The adult, generally the parent, may sing and rock the child. Movement, sound, and rhythm, as well as color and shapes, are important elements in the child's world and are imperative to perceptual sensory development, and understanding of the world and culture. The parents may decorate the child's environment in colors and shapes, and point out various visual manifestations in the close confines of the home and further into their cultural world. The infant develops the multi-senses it has been blessed with, the senses of sight, hearing, smell, taste, and touch. Perception and interpretation are enhanced through developed senses. Multi-sensory perception is developed through expression and frequent use of alternate forms of communication. I believe understanding is enhanced through sensitive, multi-sensory perception.

Play is a natural element in a child's motor, sensory, cultural, and intellectual development. Children begin to play long before they can communicate effectively with words. Through play, they express their ideas, moods, and personalities to others. In play, children learn about their world through imitation, repetition, and interpretation. The use of dramatic play organizes human experience and information, and clarifies human emotions such as desire, conflict, and reconciliation.

Children leap for joy, chase or crouch in feigned fright, stamp in anger, and run in circles. Anthropologists have described these heightened and stylized movements as dance, which they consider an instinct, for dancing is universal.

Every culture, age, and race has dance as a means of social expression and to satisfy the instinct for play. The way a culture dances, whether the dance be official, traditional, religious, or popular, indicates much about the way individuals in the culture feel and live their lives.

Some time after infancy, and into western-culture school age, humans as sensing, feeling beings are trained to become less sensitive to natural and manmade phenomena. The individual's value in society is based on the ability to regurgitate and manipulate words and numbers. Children, in most schools, are force-fed dead information with such haste that there is no time left for play in the sand box, imitating the behavior of adults, individuals and animals in their experiential environment. Times to be cradled and sung to by nurturing adults, listening to exaggerated story-telling, becoming aware of and dabbling with color, line, shape, form, and human expression become limited or nonexistent. Why has there been a shift in emphasis from sound, image, and gesture as ways of perceiving, expressing, and communicating with others to a primary focus on word and number? The technological mindset emphasizes science, technology, and other forms of mechanical thinking, ruled by word and number. This mindset has encouraged the twentieth century western people to divorce their minds from their senses and their bodies and to ignore or reject the information received through them. This attitude has reduced, ignored the importance of, devalued the recognition of, or otherwise rejected the elements that make humans different from all other living and mechanical beings. Furthermore, it is equally disconcerting that western cultures have forgotten why multi-sensory perception, expression, and communication were once important to human existence and survival, and how they gave personal meaning to life.

I believe that as a culture, we have forgotten the ways, means, and reasons to take care of the human body, mind, and soul. Personal and group culture, and cross-cultural well-being and understanding have all suffered.

The Student

When I was a child, I played as a child. The world was mine to experience through my senses. I ran and played, and sang and danced, and created with my friends, neighborhood children, and the various animals of my acquaintance.

I was fortunate to have lived next to a family with six boys, in a small Manitoba town. It had bushes and trees to build forts and tree-houses, a sand pit to swim in and catch frogs during hot summer days, hills to slide on, and snow to build and tunnel through. The neighbor boys were free spirits; my parents called them wild! As soon as the frost disappeared from the ground, we were getting our bare feet tempered for the hot summer sun: wading through the cool spring water in ditches, determining the depth of the water as it flooded over the rim of our rubber boots, stepping in oozing mud which squished between our toes, or leaving footprints on warm summer sand. It was a great life before I turned six!

All the ways I had experienced life and learned were through my senses. Once in school, the freedom of discovery through the senses was not encouraged. We were given facts from the teachers and the textbooks. The information was never discussed, inquiry and questioning were not tolerated. My time in school became waiting time.

One bright moment on the first day of school was when I met the most beautiful girl I had ever seen. Barbara was petite, and had black hair, and deep brown eyes. We became best friends immediately! We had great adventures discovering and digging clay to mold with, hay to build houses with, and mice to tame. These and other adventures continued for years when the school day was over, on weekends, and for many summers at her parents' farm. Later that first fall, I met Karen. Although a year younger than I, she was an accomplished dress designer, an architect, and interior designer. We designed and built to our hearts' content! We scrounged through her mother's sewing basket and came up with wonderfully textured and colored fabrics. There was not a poorly dressed doll or cut-out within our grasp. When her small bedroom became too crowded for our fantastic ideas, we ventured outdoors to create and build. Scrap boards became the raw material for our unique house designs. We often debated about placements for entrance ways, traffic areas, size of rooms, and natural lighting. It was great fun!

The worst part about turning six years old was that my time to play, sing and dance, create, and discover my world was limited! I had to sit in one of those ugly brown desks, with green cast iron legs which were welded together in rows. We had to sit "straight up," often on our hands, face forward, and listen to the teacher at the front of the classroom. Sometimes the teacher talked about birds and animals, or frogs and fish, but we never ventured out of the classroom. We never looked upon, touched, smelled, or tasted what we were expected to understand. The imagination was never intentionally called into action.

I was rarely eager for the teacher's attention. Awareness of the individual student in the class by the teacher usually came in the form of "trial by question." The questions always required only one right answer and no imagination. Before my first year was over, I learned the rules of the game of schooling. I always chose, and sometimes had to fight for, a seat at the back of the room. The "back of the room" students were generally boys, who were equally disenchanted with school life. My preference in desks, however, was not only at the rear of the room, but was the one by the window where I could look out, and day-dream, waiting for the moment the bell would ring. The bell would mark the time when I could escape and continue my adventures on the snowy hillside, catch tadpoles at the sand pit, or watch the sand swallows hatch from their eggs, or be fed as young birds.

Not all the classroom moments were horrible. My "claim to fame" in the school classroom was that I could draw. I loved Friday afternoon when we were given part of an hour, some paper and crayons, and allowed, in most cases, to draw whatever we wanted. Often fellow students would ask me to draw part of their pictures for them – the parts they had difficulty with, like the legs on a horse, or the face of cat. This gave me great pleasure, not to mention praise, from my teachers, fellow classmates, and parents. It helped me to endure the time I spent sitting in the small brown desk with cast iron legs, deciphering the language of word and number.

We never moved from our desks, except to hand the teacher our work for correction. We never danced during school time, and the only songs we ever sang or heard were "O'Canada" and "God Save the Queen."

When I was a child, was it a happy time? Yes, definitely! I was happiest on Friday afternoons when we got colored paper and crayons, at 3:30 when the bell would ring announcing the end of the school day, and on Saturdays, Sundays, and summer holiday time, when I could continue my adventures by myself or with my friends.

I have some fond memories of a few teachers who touched my thoughts and intellect. They were teachers who encouraged my questions and praised my talents. However, most of the teaching in my public school educational experience was thoughtless. The teachers followed the myth that learning can be guaranteed if instruction is delivered systematically, one small piece at a time, with frequent tests to ensure that students and teachers stayed on task (Smith, 1986). Most teachers failed to encourage the love of questioning and learning and the use of multi-sensory modes of information gathering, communication, and expression. Rote memory was applauded, and questioning students had no place in the teacher-directed classroom.

I firmly believe that meaningful learning and teaching prevails in environments where multi-sensory perceptive modes of information gathering, expression, and communication are promoted and encouraged. This is where the art of play, dramatics, movement, sound, rhythm, shaping of space, line, and color have a profound influence on the intellectual and social development of children.

The Teacher

I didn't become a teacher for altruistic reasons. It wasn't because I wanted to make the world a better place for children! Not in the beginning of my teaching career. I discovered that school was an acceptable place as long as I could teach art. However, my first teaching assignment was to teach social studies as well as art in a "tough" junior high school. I faced students who leaned back in their chairs, with arms crossed in front of them, as if to say, "I dare you to teach me!" As a first year teacher, I tried to model my teaching to the methods used by the other teachers in the school. Before class started, I wrote notes on the blackboard in order to free me to keep an eye on the students and not have my back turned to them. These students were accomplished at making spit-balls and shooting them accurately across the room! I had the students copy these meaningless notes neatly into their notebooks. I noticed that some teachers in this school kept the off-task students seated at the back of the room with a message, "don't bother me, and I won't bother you." These and other methods of non-teaching I could not accept! Many Fridays I went home frustrated, exhausted, and not sure I wanted to return to the classroom on Monday morning. However, as time passed by, my understanding of the students as a group and as individuals with problems and needs began to develop. I felt insecure in my ability to teach them to read and write, and in many instances it appeared that the school system had already given up on these children. Many were destined for vocational schools when they reached thirteen, or were expected to eventually drop out of school entirely. Gradually, I discovered I had something to offer these children in the art room. What I could offer them was success, safety, enjoyment, and personal satisfaction. I tried to transfer these feelings into the social studies classroom. I even secretly moved the social studies class into the art room where the students could build, color, and design projects developed from the social studies curriculum. I am happy to say these ideas are not new to teaching, but they were to me in my first teaching assignment.

As I became knowledgeable about teaching art to children, I also recognized the importance of all the arts to the social, emotional, and intellectual development of children. It is important to learn and experience, and develop personal meaning or perspective through the multi-senses of sight, sound, image, and movement. Furthermore, it is of benefit for all to develop the ability to express what they think and feel through thoughtful multisensory response.

I discovered I could have "Friday arts afternoons" with the students everyday! We could investigate and experiment with color, line, shape, rhythm, movement, balance, display, composition, proportion, mood, feeling, expression, and imagination, in the art room, the music room, the dance studio, or the drama theatre!

I believe it is difficult not only for children, but for all learners, to learn or comprehend, to investigate or question, when the information they are receiving is unrelated to their life and is presented, communicated, and expressed only through word and number. This form of non-inquiry, or forgotten thoughtfulness, does not develop or use the multi-sensory modes of information gathering, perceiving, and expression. The learning environments should be filled with images, sounds, smells, movement, temperatures, animal and plant, and human life forms, for humans are multi-sensing learners.

According to Brown (1987), the best way to restore balance to a system that is too heavily tilted toward the basics would be to create a strong counter-culture within the system which would value inquiry and thoughtfulness above all else. In my many years of teaching in various schools, I have seen pockets of this counterculture described by Brown created within the educational system. This is a counterculture which values not only inquiry with the use of word and number, but the thoughtful inquiry and perplexity which require multi-sensory modes of information gathering, communicating, and express-ing. I have seen evidence of and have experienced thoughtful learning and teaching, especially in special needs schools and environments, where teachers were encouraged to work across curricular subject areas, through integration with other subjects, or with and among the fine arts.

I experienced encouragement from school administrators and fellow staff members when I was teaching students who were considered "different." Labels for these students varied. They were students who were identified as learning disabled, gifted and talented, deaf, blind, delinquent, or new to my country and had not yet learned to speak and understand English. The "traditional" teacher at the front of the classroom did not reach or find success with these special children. These teachers seemed to consider the curriculum content more important than the child. When adaptation did not occur, the "traditional" teacher did not survive for any length of time in those educational environments where the children were "different." It appeared that the teachers in these "schools with a difference" realized the need, or were encouraged to teach, with the "child at the centre" instead of the material or curriculum. Other more thoughtful ways of education were attempted using the multi-senses for information gathering and communication.

A Classroom Vignette

Thoughtfulness is a condition in which a person or group is absorbed in thought and may be characterized by careful, reasoned thinking (Brown, 1987). I believe careful, reasoned thinking requires the assistance of multi-sensory modes of information gathering and communication. There are barriers in the educational system which hamper instruction conducive to thoughtfulness

(Brown, 1988). These barriers are embedded in the expectations and assumptions of teachers, administrators, parents, and students.

The most frequent rationale for not offering education conducive to thoughtfulness includes time, curriculum coverage, and testing. Many educators feel there is not enough time to plan, or the time is too fragmented to allow for sustained reading, writing, discussion. There is not enough time for experiences and investigation in the arts, or thoughtful projects, question solving, or multi-sensory activities. There is the belief that there is not enough time to "waste" on playing with the multi-sensory methods of understanding the world. Time is driven by the "imperatives of coverage. . . . Teachers feel they must cover an already sprawling and constantly expanding list of topics within and across subject-matter fields" (Brown, 1988, p. 5). The conviction that higher literacies cannot be measured in ways compatible, in whole or in part, with current accountability systems is another constraint.

I believe there are ways for teachers and schools to develop more thoughtful environments for learning and teaching and to overcome the barriers to thoughtfulness. The best examples come from some of the fine work that teachers in many elementary and special-needs schools are attempting to accomplish. The teachers in these situations may be the first to be truly thoughtful in learning and teaching, since they are free from many of the constraints of curriculum and testing, and focus more on a "student-centred approach."

The following is a description of an elementary school setting where the teachers overcame the barriers to thoughtful education, where students were encouraged to learn, communicate and express using their multi-sensory abilities. I wish to describe the work of thoughtful teachers who were encouraged to develop unique teaching strategies, and the thoughtful classrooms they developed.

A group of dedicated elementary core and fine arts specialists joined efforts in creating an educational experience for a group of students in grades four through six in their care. The barriers to thoughtfulness described by Brown were overcome, and the arts enhanced the questioning, learning, understanding, and demonstration of learning for the students.

The Alberta Department of Education stipulates what students should learn in their years in public school. In looking specifically at the social studies curriculum, various grade levels include study of a particular country or culture. The study of a country or culture cannot be undertaken effectively without emphasis on the arts of the people which make up the group. The group of teachers involved in this thoughtful project decided to start with the study of Greece, the birthplace of western civilization, government, science, mathematics, education, architecture, and the fine arts. They set out to develop resources to enhance the understanding of a culture through the fine arts. The teachers were enthusiastic with the plans for an integrated curriculum of studies on Greece. The primary task was to organize the curriculum rather than to add or subtract from it.

According to Brown (1987), many teachers fear thoughtfulness in the classroom because it cannot be easily controlled, too much time is lost, and the required material may not be covered. Therefore, a thoughtful environment must be provided for teachers and students. Teachers need an opportunity to share, dialogue, reflect, and observe thoughtful instruction of exemplary practice in order to create and sustain the desired environment. Thoughtfulness is developed through experience more than through lecture, through practice more than passivity (Brown,1989).

The teachers involved in this Greek study were definitely thoughtful educators. They had the ability to work in teams, were flexible, had a strong belief in self-directed learning, and understood the importance of the fine and performing arts to cultural understanding and appreciation. Furthermore, the teachers were in agreement with Wiggins (1989) that curriculum is inseparable from assessment. The course of studies was organized around essential questions and culminated in a public exhibition and performance of mastery.

The teaching practices in this classroom did not follow the myth that learning can be guaranteed if instruction is delivered systematically, one small piece at a time, with frequent tests to ensure students and teachers stay on task (Smith, 1986). Instead, the motto could have been : "nullius in verba," or "take nobody's word for it, see it for yourself." Knowledge must solve a problem or provoke inquiry for it to seem important, and teachers must equip students to keep questioning (Wiggins,1989). It was not possible to write scope and sequence lesson plans in advance. Just as Wiggins had hoped, the text books, if there were any, became reference books. The students designed the questions and the tasks which became their final presentation. The best questions, according to Wiggins (1989), come from engaged students, and this project proved he was right. The students became experts on an aspect of the topic "Greece" and learned to collaborate with other students, exchanging important information. According to Brown (1989), thoughtfulness is a constructive, not a passive, undertaking.

The students were introduced to the study of Greece by being asked what they already knew about the topic. The students shared their knowledge with each other, creating mind maps and webbing. All the information was gathered in an attempt to organize it into categories such as architecture, mythology, philosophy, astronomy, mathematics, politics, athletics, and so forth. The students then broke into small discussion groups to share further and write down ideas from different areas they might wish to explore. The students were then asked by their teacher-advisors which of the questions they found most interesting. Dillon (1983) says there are two types of questions – everyday questions and educative questions. To conceive an educative question requires thought; to formulate it requires labor; to pose it, tact. These thoughtful, tactful students labored to formulate their essential questions.

The teachers discussed in this vignette believe children learn best when they are interested in what they are doing. According to an article in Horace (1990), asking questions as a way of organizing content serves to strengthen students' sense of their own authority over content. Students love to learn, and these teachers got excited about learning as well, producing a constant dialogue. The teachers felt they learned as much as the students. This form of teaching required strong self-concept on the part of the teacher who is not the "full-frontal" or "traditional" teacher.

The student formed his or her own questions. The teachers did not abdicate their role as teacher-guide-coach and intervened when it was best for the student. The students then read, looked at pictures, slides, filmstrips, listened to music, drew pictures, developed models. They became experts on an aspect of the theme. Students needed to decide what the final product would be or look like, or what the form of their presentation of mastery of learning would take. These decisions affected their research, what expertise they required, time and material needed. The students' studies led them to problems of mathematics, politics, astronomy, architecture, mythology, science, government, the Olympics, and of course, dance, drama, art and music. The correlation of subjects helped the students develop awareness of the relationship and connection between the subjects and disciplines. When the students were not working on their Greek research questions in the library, their classroom, or the science lab, they were learning to sing songs from Greece as well as learn at least one Greek dance. They created their own plays based on a Greek myth or character. All the students chose to be a particular god, goddess, monster, or other mythical creature for the planned evening celebration. Students created symbols illustrating the nature of their character, and costumes. They illustrated Greek myths using colored paper, pen and ink, pastels, clay, papier-mâché, or paint. They created relief murals and Greek pottery.

An exhibition of mastery should be the students' opportunity to show off what they know and are able to do rather than a "trial by question" (Sizer, 1984). According to Wiggins (1989), an exhibition challenges students to show off not merely their knowledge but their initiative, problem posing and solving of their own design. Students who have to exhibit their knowledge and skills get learning into their bones; an active learner becomes a lifelong learner (Brown, 1989).

The core and fine arts teachers working with the students on this project decided the exhibition would take two forms – a classroom presentation of the investigation and a public performance in the evening. The classroom presentations were varied with the assistance of overheads, maps in two dimensions and relief, models, posters, puppets, music, writings, artifacts, dance, plays, and artistic creations, all used to help the students illustrate their investigations. The students learned many things when they shared in this manner. The teachers felt that students do not learn in order to keep the learning to themselves. They learn in order to share. After the classroom presentation, students wrote a project evaluation on their work and the work of their fellow classmates. According to Brown (1987), accountability systems for thoughtfulness will require new kinds of assessments requiring multiple indicators of quality. The problem of accountability only arises when someone wants to put numbers on learning and compare how much is learned (Smith, 1986). The students were asked to evaluate their own learning and performance.

The study ended in the celebration of a Greek Festival. On this evening, the students dressed as Greek gods, goddesses, and mythical creatures. They performed their student-developed plays using props and backdrops they had designed. The students sang, played musical instruments, and danced. Parents and relatives filled the gymnasium to capacity. Art works and the humanities projects from the class presentations were displayed in the main hallways, with student creators standing by to answer queries. After the performance, guests and performers indulged in Greek dessert and lemon drink. The students experienced, manipulated, and created the arts and ideas of Greece. The students, teachers, and parents developed a greater understanding through multi-sensory modes of information gathering, expression, and communication. According to all involved, a greater crosscultural and cross- disciplinary understanding was achieved. The trick to good schooling is not just to meet minimum standards (Sizer, 1984). In authentic performance, the student knows the nature of the challenge ahead of time, as with an athletic or artistic event (Wiggins, 1989). The recital, debate, play or game is the heart of the matter, the authentic performance.

The learning and teaching experience just described was personally and academically rewarding for the teachers and students involved. The teachers encouraged the opportunity to observe and share, to gather information using the multi-senses, to stimulate and foster active inquiry, and to use multi-sensory modes of communication and expression. Coverage of required curriculum was not a constraint, nor was the time spent on the topic of investigation. These teachers and students overcame the barriers to thoughtfulness. Thoughtful learning and teaching prevailed in this environment where perceptive modes of information gathering, questioning, inquiry, expression, and communication were promoted, encouraged and became part of the learning environment.

This is but one vignette or "slice of life" from a thoughtful classroom. Over the years, I have had the pleasure of seeing and being a part of thoughtful learning and teaching, and I believe this will continue. This past week a very bright, wonderful, grade ten student told me she would like to become a teacher when she finishes her formal schooling. At one time in my life, I may have tried to discourage her by saying: "Why waste your brains and talent in teaching! It's a dead end job with little reward." I did not say these things, for I now have confidence in the future of education. Furthermore, I can with total honesty tell not only this young girl, but also my nineteen-year-old son, and whoever is searching for a fulfilling career, that the field of education is the direction to take.

Sharon Gibb is presently a coordinator-instructor in the Bachelor of Education program at Mount Royal College in Calgary. She completed an undergraduate degree in education at the University of Alberta and a master's degree in leadership from Brigham Young University. Sharon received her Ed.D. degree from Brigham Young University in 1992. Sharon is the author of twenty-one books for students, teachers, and parents in the area of health education and personal development. She is currently co-authoring a teacher education text for use in post-secondary institutions. With twenty years of teaching experience in public and post-secondary schools in Alberta, Sharon continues to speak and be involved with curriculum development for provincial education departments in Canada. She is also a senator with the University of Calgary.

7

I'm Thinking of Leaving Teaching

Sharon Gibb

The following two letters are an account of two teachers: one who is planning to leave teaching because of a thoughtless school environment, and the other who defends teaching. Through this dialogue, both teachers are forced to examine their perception of teaching.

Dear Sharon,

It has been two years since I was enrolled in your philosophy of education course at the university. Since that time, I have been teaching at a large urban junior high school. I want you to know that I am planning to leave the profession after this school year, in spite of all your encouragement about thoughtful teaching and learning, and the difference teachers can make in the lives of students. I find the profession, the students, and their parents to be thoughtless. All my friends support my decision to leave teaching, as they too feel that thoughtful teaching and learning are not appreciated. I do not have an answer for them, and if I can not think of a good reason to stay in teaching, I will quit.

Rhonda

Dear Rhonda,

In response to your letter about thoughtful teaching and learning, I would like to share with you a recent trip my daughter and I had to a country farmers' market. What does a farmers' market have to do with thoughtful teaching? As I depict the thoughts of educational scholars, and describe the answers to related questions of thoughtful teaching and learning, I will let you be the judge of how this all relates to the farmers' market.

We arrived at exactly 8:00 A.M. to be the first people at the market, but to our chagrin, the parking field was overflowing with cars. We hurriedly made our way through the field to the booths where customers were swarming over the tables of fresh vegetables, fruits, and crafts. There were hundreds of tables and the message was the same at all of them – don't ask questions, but buy, buy, buy. I was caught in the maze of people and the frenzy of buying something, anything, before the merchandise was all gone. The question of whether I needed the item never surfaced; everyone was buying, so it must be needed. In fact, I held several twenty dollar bills in my hand to save time from having to open and close my purse. I definitely had caught the fever.

Then my daughter spotted a small booth set in the background between two very busy tables of crafts and vegetables. A boy of about eight or nine, with the most determined look I had ever seen, sat behind a display of small boards he had painted and nailed crudely together to resemble airplanes and bombers. These were his wares: airplanes, and the vision of their intent was obvious to all those who could take time to stop for a moment. My daughter tugged at my arm and attempted to persuade me to relinquish three ripe tomatoes. I pretended to respond with, "Oh, that's nice." But I never saw the booth, the child, or the airplanes. Again she pointed him out until finally my eyes focused on the minute object in this "humongous" market.

I looked at the boy. First his determination caught my attention, then his airplanes, and then his vision. He was selling more than airplanes. Amidst the commotion, here was one person who truly had something to sell: "My airplanes are like eagles. Do you ever watch how high eagles soar?" Interestingly enough, he never talked of price or the features of his craft; those items were irrelevant now that his question had been asked.

What next? Well, my daughter and I attempted to answer his question in this most unusual learning environment. We then responded with our own curiosity: Where did you get the idea? How long did they take you to build? How old are you? Did anyone help you? How is business? Where do you live? What's your name? The boy replied as a great teacher would; he answered our questions with caring ones of his own: Why do you want to buy my airplane? Do you like airplanes? Is this plane for you? As we paid Samuel the two dollars for a paint-splattered yellow and red bomber made from three small boards, I realized that we had just purchased part of his vision, wondered if we could fulfil the dream, and realized that we had just made a friend. Although he was just eight, he had been our teacher.

As I drove back into the city, I wrestled with the concept of thoughtful teaching and learning and your letter. This boy had captured the essence of my response. In reality, schools are like farmers' markets: there is a product to sell, customers, and interaction. In both situations, it is rarely expected that the customer will question the product; everyone is buying it, so it must be needed. The teacher and the vendor have a job to do: one has a curriculum to follow and student tests to administer as their measure; the other has a product to sell and a profit to represent success.

Prior to this incident, I had pondered the indicators of thoughtfulness, but it was only after today that I realized I had formed some strong feelings for thoughtful teaching and learning. To begin, thoughtfulness is how we perceive human beings; it is an engagement of the heart and the head. A teacher cannot teach unless he or she is cognizant of the emotional and mental abilities of the student (Barell, 1991). For example, you cannot fill the registry of the mind unless the student is engaged in the learning process, and he or she will not be engaged in the learning process unless the emotional, social and spiritual self is addressed. As Samuel talked to us about his airplanes, he made us feel confident with our questions and ourselves and therefore we dared to risk. A thoughtful teacher never forgets the "heart" of the pupil.

Furthermore, the word "confidence" is vital to thoughtfulness. Stemming from this base of confidence-building, it is gratifying to note the possible end-products of teaching and learning – having a vision, developing an inquiring mind, and formulating a disposition to follow a curiosity without fear of taking risks. This provides the setting for doing humanely the work of the mind (Brown,1987). Had Samuel started with the price of his airplanes and an outline of their features, we might have listened politely, perhaps even purchased one as a novelty, but certainly teaching and learning would have been minimal. However, Samuel was a thoughtful teacher. He had a vision, he engaged us immediately with a question, secured our confidence, made us think, and then sparked our curiosity. Interestingly enough, I doubt that Samuel would ever describe himself as our teacher. So it is with thoughtful teachers; they are as much learners as they are teachers. Perhaps we put too much emphasis on teaching or telling others what we know, and not enough on learning or listening. For this reason we skew our worth as teachers.

What is a teacher worth? All the current research today is unable to address this question. However, I believe our worth is directly related to the transfer of ownership in the learning environment. Ownership begins when one is "sparked" with curiosity. My twenty years of teaching experience have told me that when this spark occurs, the student is in the fledgling stages of displaying some ownership, or feeling part of the learning situation. There is now a collaborative effort between teacher and student. Without this quality of ownership, it is impossible for any lasting learning to occur.

So how do we establish ownership? Ownership is a natural experience in learning; it evolves as a result of an active, hands-on, whole approach, of allowing thinking, problem-solving and creativity to be enhanced, and encouraged. Yet many teachers, for whatever reason, prefer a teacher-directed approach to teaching, such as lecturing. The teacher most often stands at the front of a class and tells the students what they should know. Goodlad (1984) claims that 80 percent of learning occurs in this one-way learning environment. I try to encourage ownership from my college students, and I employ a variety of thoughtful classroom activities to accomplish this task. However, several of my colleagues prefer to lecture, and have judged my efforts to be more of novelty than teaching, for they question: What about measurement? I contend that not all factors in teaching can be measured, nor are they visible to the untrained eye.

This notwithstanding, there are other qualities of teaching and learning that we intuitively recognize as being thoughtful. They are difficult to describe. However, we all seem to recognize them when we see them. Perhaps it has to do with "caring" and "loving." For I believe it is in the ambience of these emotions that we recognize thoughtful teaching. Sacalis (1991), an educator from Romania, embellished this thought while claiming that first teachers have to display some human qualities such as loving and caring, then learning begins. Why do some teachers have an impact on us? Why do some teachers make a difference in our lives? I believe, as with Samuel, that we recognize thought-fulness in the mannerisms of the teachers, their voices, their body language, their ambience in the learning environment, their attitudes, their enthusiasm for the subject, their willingness to share and to listen, and their patience to allow learning to happen. Brown (1991) supports these thoughts. He defines thought-fulness as being characterized by careful, reasoned thinking, in combination with consideration of others, and being selflessly concerned with the needs of others. Thoughtful teaching and learning, then, goes back to my earlier premise of how we view human beings.

Another quality of a thoughtful teacher which has intuitive overtones is that aspect of being effortless; we should not have to think about our actions if they are cradled in caring and loving, otherwise we are not truly thoughtful. However, at the beginning, like riding a bicycle, there is a learning period or at least a thinking period that one encounters. For example in teaching, I find the following actions of the thoughtful teacher to become effortless over time: acknowledging students by name instead of pointing; considering all answers to questions instead of noting only right and wrong responses; portraying body language that encourages learning instead of standing securely behind a po-dium; displaying personal enthusiasm for wanting to teach instead of showing the drudgery of having to teach; being knowledgeable about what is being taught rather than putting in time; eagerly accepting learning challenges rather than being insulted when a lack of knowledge is disclosed; having a concern for the education of the whole child, the mental, physical, emotional, social and spiritual, rather than being purely concerned with the registry of the mind.

And yet, society is making teachers accountable through testing to ensure that the registry is filled. Therefore we have become somewhat paranoid with success, and we have equated success in teaching by being able to measure how much information we can cause a student to put into his or her brain. We have become afraid to just talk or discuss in class, or to allow students to elude the curriculum. As stated earlier, questioning and gaining ownership for learning are essential characteristics of thoughtfulness (Brown,1987). Wiggins (1989) supports this thought in that he believes good teaching is not test or curriculum driven, it is meaning driven. This places teachers in a most difficult position. The question is: Can we be characterized as thoughtful if our only concern is for the registry of the mind? I think not. As I mentioned earlier, thoughtful teachers wish to educate the whole child. Therefore, I suggest we do the job we are hired to do, to teach a subject matter to children, but do so in the context of thoughtfulness. How can this be accomplished in a society that is technologically driven? Is the present mindset of society technologically driven? Few educators would refute the concept that society is the driving force behind what is taught in education. When the Soviet Union launched Sputnik into space in 1957, the people in North America questioned our schools for the ability to do the same. Our frame of reference in society is against thoughtful learning – it strongly favors controlled curriculum, examinations, timetables; there is no time for questions. However, it has long been established that it is questioning that drives real learning. Because the concept of testing and measurement is constantly at the forefront of education, we continually ask ourselves: How do we measure good questions? Can evaluation be overlooked in an empirical society where the technological mindset requires fragmentation of ideas into parts which can be justified, supported, and therefore easily measured? This in itself can result in part of the frustration for leaving teaching. Had Samuel been forced to examine how much we knew about airplanes before he sold us one, we would not have bought the product. At that point in our learning, we were certainly not motivated to buy his airplane.

But Samuel knew where he was headed; he had a vision. Perhaps this is indicative of entrepreneurs. In order to survive in the business world, personal goals and philosophies are encouraged as a driving force. Yet, in education, we fear establishing our goals and philosophies. As you remember in my university course, I stated a personal philosophy of education during the first day of the semester. To refresh your memory, I believe in three values in teaching: education of the whole child, education in the context of being value-based, and education for thinking. What is your philosophy? Can you stand up for what you believe or will you allow someone else to dictate your thoughts and vision?

If you have formulated your educational beliefs, then I have anticipated your next questions: Can teachers be taught how to be thoughtful? If thoughtfulness can be taught, can all the characteristics be taught, or just a few? Resnick (1987) describes skill development in relation to thinking, and believes that thinking skills can be taught. Then there is Solway (1989), who uses the word "training" for skill development, and notes that "you can train a dog, but you must educate a man" (p. 36). In order to teach, we must know the qualities of that which we wish to teach. If we can agree on one, two, or more indicators for thoughtfulness, then it is my opinion we can teach people to be thoughtful teachers. Like Brown (1991)[1], I believe there are distinct indicators for a climate conducive to a literacy of thoughtful education. Stated simply, I have identified them as the "Three I's" – indicators of teaching and learning:

1. Ensure that you are a master in your content area so as to develop a passion for what you teach. Samuel's passion for airplanes was the catalyst for my daughter and I learning about the subject. As the teacher develops this passion for what is taught, the student experiences the beginning stages of learning with the transfer of a knowledge base or *Information.*

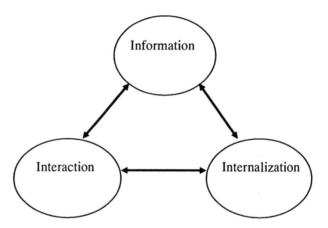

2. Allow your students to react to the information. This could occur in a variety of manners such as: reading more, discussing the thoughts with others, interviewing others, answering questions, and writing. We learned about airplanes because the teacher and students had an interchange of questions. This is the *Interaction* phase.

3. Now comes the essential phase of *Internalization.* Students must be given time to make sense of what they have learned and to personalize the thoughts. We walked away from Samuel and his booth with three paint-spattered boards which represented my teacher's dream, our acquisition of captured knowledge, and our eagerness to share our learning with others.

It now appears to me that if indicators of thoughtfulness can be identified, the next natural question is: Why are schools not more thoughtful? Perhaps the answer is related to the following reasons: it is easier to develop tests that ask questions than it is to deal with opinions and complicated matters; thoughtfulness cannot be easily controlled; time is a factor, you can lose track of what the required material is to be; and teachers are held accountable for the minimums and basics (Brown, 1987). As well, the factor of teacher education needs to be addressed. For even though teachers like yourself may perceive what they aspire to have happen in the classroom, most teachers do not know how to incorporate active learning, critical and creative thinking, problem solving, and inquiry. If teachers could be taught the skills of thoughtfulness in their education classes, would this then be the answer? Although we talked about thoughtful teaching and learning in my education philosophy course, we did not pursue the skills of thoughtfulness in the classroom. For as you know, the curriculum dictates what was taught – an example of thoughtlessness. Perhaps the qualities of thoughtlessness require examination.

I have discussed in this letter what is thoughtfulness, but I have not dwelled on what is not thoughtful. The following Dickens (1961) example illustrates the meaning of thoughtlessness and the very reason our students and teachers give-up on schooling. Thomas Gradgrind is a person of exactness – there is no room for error, flexibility, thinking, or practical reality.

> Thomas Gradgrind, sir. A man of realities. A man of facts and calculations. A man who proceeds upon the principle that two and two are four, and nothing over, and who is not to be talked into allowing for anything over. Thomas Gradgrind, sir – peremptorily Thomas – Thomas Gradgrind. With a rule and a pair of scales, and the multiplication table always in his pocket, sir, ready to weigh and measure any parcel of human nature, and tell you exactly what it comes to. It is a mere question of figures, a case of simple arithmetic. You might hope to get some other nonsensical belief into the head of . . . Thomas Gradgrind – no sir ! (p. 12)

How may I persuade you to remain in teaching? I cannot. However, I would like to leave you with one additional thought. I believe we need to become like Samuel the teacher – making teaching effortless and avoiding the all-consuming preciseness of Thomas Gradgrind. So, no matter what you may choose to do in life, the fact remains that you care about teaching and learning. Therefore, you will naturally foster learning in whatever circumstance you have a pupil, whether it be at a farmers' market, over a telephone, or in a formal classroom. Perhaps this is the answer to the dilemma of education – the classroom is not the only environment for teaching and learning.

Thoughtfully yours,
Sharon Gibb.

Notes

[1]* Physical classroom environment (reference materials, student work on display)

* Interaction between student and teacher (Is it teacher talk? Does the teacher allow sufficient time for responses? Does the teacher appear to be the learner?)

* Questioning strategies (Do questions call for analysis, synthesis, interpretation or evaluation? Do questions drive students toward deeper understanding? Does the teacher encourage students to ask questions?)

* Amount of facilitation and probing (Do students feel encouraged to expand or clarify ideas? Does the teacher provide conceptual bridges to help students move from present understanding to new understanding?)

* Discussion element (Do teacher and students synthesize or summarize during the discussion? Is there sufficient time for good discussion?)

* Nonverbal indicators or engagement (How many students are alert or engaged?)

* Courtesy and sensitivity (Do teacher and students listen carefully, use polite speech and acknowledge and support one another's views? Are conflicting views accepted? Does the teacher praise students for their responses or help lead them from incorrect to correct perceptions?)

* Amount of reflection or self-regulation (Are students able to describe their thinking or problem-solving strategies? If students take notes, what do they intend to do with them?)

* Risk-taking environment (Is there a general acceptance of a healthy amount of uncertainty or ambiguity? Do students explore or brainstorm? Are students encouraged to make mistakes and learn from them?)

(Brown, 1991, pp. xiv, xv)

HOPE

Judy Hehr is presently the Assistant Principal at Catherine Nichols Gunn Elementary School in Calgary, Alberta. She completed an undergraduate degree at the University of Calgary, specializing in Early Childhood Education, a Master of Arts in Administration from Gonzaga University, and a graduate diploma in computer applications at the University of Calgary. Judy received her Ed.D. degree from Brigham Young University in 1992. She is a strong believer in student-centred education. She and her husband, Dick, who is also a teacher, live in Calgary. They have a son, Kent, and a daughter, Kristie.

8

A Web of Understanding

Judy Hehr

Mount Royal College hockey player Kent Hehr, 21, was last night upgraded from critical to serious condition in the Foothills Hospital. The shooting came after a vehicle with two occupants chased the car in which Hehr was a passenger for 15 blocks. When the cars reached the 4900 block of Crowchild Trail south at 2:50 A.M., a shot was fired from a small calibre handgun. "The bullet went right through Hehr's neck as he sat in the car's front passenger seat," said Inspector Randy Cottrell. "The slug caught the victim in the throat and severely damaged his spinal cord as it passed through." "This appears to be a random senseless shooting," said Inspector Ray McBrien.

Calgary Sun, October 3, 1991

Kent is my son. On October 3, 1991, as a result of the shot through his neck, he became a quadriplegic. Initially, survival was questionable. For two days following the accident, Kent was able to breathe on his own. However, on the third day, breathing became so labored that the doctors ventilated his lungs by inserting a tube down his nose. His vital functions were assisted by tubes and monitored by machines which were continually beeping. There was no guarantee that Kent would ever be able to breathe on his own again. Anguish, fear, anger, and grief enveloped our family.

Why have I chosen to share this story? Until October 3, my life had proceeded in a fairly orderly fashion. I was a mother, a wife, a friend, a teacher, and a community member. In recent years, a major focus in my life was achieving my doctorate. Since the shooting, my thoughts and feelings have totally centred around the change our family is experiencing. This essay becomes my opportunity to share thoughts and feelings – attempting from the context of my continuing education to make meaning of what has happened. Bruner (1990) reinforces the importance of our stories:

> Narrativizing makes the happening comprehensible against the background of ordinariness we take as the basic state of life . . . I have wanted to make it clear that our capacity to render experience in terms of narrative is not just child's play, but an instrument for making meaning that dominates much of life in culture. (p. 97)

The key to understanding lies in making sense of our everyday lives. So I draw on past experiences, attempting to direct, shape, and assume responsibility for my present experience, and trust this current experience to help me handle the future.

What will the future hold? There are many unknowns. The main event at the start is the experience of perplexity. That is the precondition of questioning and thus the prerequisite for learning. Questioning still might not follow, nor learning; without perplexity they cannot follow . . . Perplexity is experiencing a degree, minor or great, of doubt, wonderment, ignorance, bafflement, incomprehension, uncertainty, puzzlement (Dillon, 1988, p. 18).

Initially, perplexity included disbelief, shock and denial. But it has led to learning; questions continuously pour forth as I strive to understand more about spinal cord injuries. In trying to answer these questions, I am expanding my understanding of the shifting paradigm, a "transcendental paradigm," meaning an overall knowledge quest that would include not only the "hardware" of physical sciences but also the "software" of philosophy and psychology and the "transcendental ware" of mystical-spiritual religion" (Wilber, 1990, p. 1). Our society has tended to ground our philosophical doctrine in science and technology for the past three hundred years. We have simplified the world into linear concepts and come to believe that there is one answer to each question (Flinders, 1990). But as I observe and learn about Kent's injuries, I know there is no one single answer.

From the scientific perspective there is a medical diagnosis. Kent is a C5 quadriplegic. "He will have use of his deltoids and biceps, but not muscle control below elbow flexors" (Maddox, 1990, p. 29). However, even this diagnosis leaves room for questions. Kent has a little feeling in one thumb which contradicts the medical diagnosis. "To put it bluntly, scientists do not deal with truth; they deal with limited and approximate descriptions of reality" (Capra, 1988, p. 48).

For forty years, my world has reinforced a belief that everything required scientific proof. Statements were significant only if they could be based on empirical evidence. But what does this scientific definition mean for the quality of Kent's life? There are C-5 quadriplegics living very limited, sometimes institutional, lives. There are also C-5 quadriplegics who are engineers, lawyers, teachers, coaches, politicians, husbands and fathers. Life expectancy continues to improve, and even at present is very close to normal. Also, technology continues to increase the possibilities both for skill development and medical improvement. Thus I embrace a new frame of reference. I adopt intuition, beliefs, feelings, and faith rather than the cold focus of science.

We are all on a journey searching for meaning. That personal journey embraces our philosophy of life.

"Philosophy begins in wonder," Plato observed, meaning that it is philosophy's task to articulate the questions arising out of the depths of the human spirit itself. Man desires knowledge of himself and his world, and it is philosophy's task to achieve such understanding. (Stewart and Mickunas, 1974, p. 5)

Initially following the shooting, I hoped someone would provide me with a clear and definitive course of action. After all, that would have fit my old paradigm of thinking. If I could succinctly define the condition, then I could isolate treatment and anticipate change. But life is not a series of discrete facts that can be isolated. Everything is not definable.

How does one begin to make sense of or decide what really counts in our lives and in our learning? We need, as Polanyi (1962) suggests, to readapt to novel and unprecedented situations: "And this is even more true of the educated mind; the capacity continually to enrich and enliven its own conceptual framework by assimilating new experience" (p. 103).

I feel so overwhelmed! A senseless act of violence has irrevocably changed our family. How do I interpret this senseless act? I begin to perceive with the help of Polanyi that doubt is my ally. "Doubt has been acclaimed not only as the touchstone of truth, but also as the safeguard of tolerance" (Polanyi, 1962, p. 271). The perpetrators of the act will probably never be found. Therefore, our family avoids the mindless activity of questioning who or why. Rather we direct our questions, energies, and resources to helping our family focus on the positive. Retribution, even on a mental level, is a negative force.

Two concepts from my doctoral work are assisting me as I attempt to thread our family's redirection in life into perspective. These concepts are thoughtfulness and change.

Thoughtfulness

In developing a working imagery of thoughtfulness, I have chosen to use the analogy of a spider's web. In constructing the most beautiful spider's web, an orb web, the spider spins several strong lines from which the web will hang. The spider then lays down the long lines from the centre of the web out to the edge, resembling the spokes of a wheel. These strong supports are needed to enable the lacy wonder to hang. Finally, the spider connects all the spokes in a spiral of sticky substance in which its food will be caught. A spider's web appears very fragile, but in actuality it is exceedingly strong.

Brown (1988) discusses thoughtfulness as a habit of the mind, Van Manen (1991) as a state of being. These two authors provide the philosophy from which my web hangs.

> Thoughtfulness is primarily a process of making meaning (not just receiving it) and negotiating it with others (not just thinking alone). It is fundamentally constructive, which is to say it derives from a different set of notions about the nature of knowledge and the process of human learning (Brown, p. 1).

> Thoughtfulness, tactfulness, is a peculiar quality that has as much to do with what we are as with what we do. It is a knowledge that issues from the heart as well as from the head. (Van Manen, p. 12)

Disposition, as explained by Katz (1988), connects the spokes of my web, as thoughtfulness to me is a disposition. It is not a fact or a skill to be learned, but rather a tendency to respond to an experience in a certain way. The disposition of thoughtfulness is the habit of my mind or the sticky substance which captures my thoughts. Continuously, I am trying to spin my web. Sometimes my thoughts make connections and form a spoke, while at other times I feel like I am floating in air, hoping, wishing, and praying. I believe thoughtfulness is not learned through instruction or drill or lectures or workbooks. I cannot give a learner a workbook on thoughtfulness and have it understood in a meaningful way. Rather, dispositions are learned primarily from being around people who have them and who exhibit them. I find myself becoming caught up in the sticky fibres of a "mystery, uncertainty, disagreement, important questions, ambiguity, curiosity" (Brown, 1991, p. 234) – conditions of thoughtfulness. My advisor and classmates are helping me connect the spokes in my web. They have become an integral part of the context in which my learning occurs. There is a sharing of experiences, ideas, and feelings. And so, the construction of meaning continues for me as a learner in my roles as mother, wife, teacher, and student.

Learning is most effective when all knowledge is structured in social context. The context creates meaning, and the meaning, in turn, creates the context. Previously, knowledge for me was an accumulation of factual, discrete information. Identification and memorization were key factors in the acquisition of knowledge. Now, integration is essential to my process of learning. And the influence of others is fundamental. Together we negotiate what it is we will accept as new knowledge. However, only I can undertake the construction of meaning for myself. "This is learning: linking prior knowledge to new knowledge within a social context" (Klinck, 1989, p. 5).

As my new learning occurs, there may be changes in vocabulary, meaning, and belief systems. Doubt and fear accompany excitement and achievement. Dissonance is also an integral feature as we move from one view of the world to another. The acquisition of new knowledge forever changes our understanding of the world around us, and presents us with new ideas and new feelings about what our future will be like (Klinck, 1989, p. 5). The enormity of the changes we are facing occasionally tempts us to embrace despair in the light of the overwhelming task ahead. But we must assume responsibility for understanding quadriplegia, rehabilitation, and determining the potential for future opportunities.

There is no single, no simple solution, only a continual searching for that which will provide optimal possibilities for all of us. Continuous inquiry is essential. Together with family and friends we ask hard questions and wrestle with difficult answers which lead to still more questions. Together we strive to make connections as the threads in the web. There are and will be pressures in any lived situation, especially during trauma. We will need to strive continuously to overcome these new challenges.

Kent is very positive, and he believes with rehabilitation he will be able to maximize his capabilities within his altered physical condition. As he explores this new world, the presence of trust is absolutely essential. Kent needs to know that his questions, answers, and experiences are all valid. They will be necessary building blocks as he strives to construct a new understanding.

> The foremost precondition for a pedagogical atmosphere is the existence of a sheltering environment of the home and the family from which the supportive feelings of trust and safety can radiate. Trust is a prerequisite for all healthy human development. (Bollnow, 1989, p. 12)

The issue of trust transcends the microcosm of our family. The internalization of the harsh reality of society's hierarchical measurement of worth has occurred. Persons with limitations experience on a daily basis the subtle and blatant prejudice implicit in the lower value they are accorded. Therefore our challenge is to be supportive of others in reflecting critically on their lifeworlds so together we will be able to articulate as persons always reaching beyond – as individuals building together, forming a common community, a community where we recognize each other's perspective and are supportive of one another, realizing that we are all learners.

> They may through their coming together constitute a newly human world, one worthy enough and responsive enough to be both durable and open to continual renewal ... Once they are open, once they are informed, once they are engaged in speech and action from their many vantage points, they may be able to identify a better state of things – and go on to transform. (Green, 1985, p. 82)

Change

In an interview with the *Calgary Herald,* November 13, 1991 Kent commented: "Priorities have changed. I was never one to cry over spilled milk. I intend to hit the books again and do better academically then I did before."

Fullan (1991) suggests that change is "a fact of life" (p. 30). Change may result because of an act of imposition, voluntary participation, or an intolerable situation. Schön (1971) suggests that change involves "passing through the zones of uncertainty . . . the situation of being lost at sea, of confronting more information than you can handle" (p. 12). Both authors speak loudly to us at present. Kent's paralysis is a fact. This new fact has placed us in a situation where we are daily encountering uncertainty.

Marris (1986) helps make meaning of the changes we are experiencing. He suggests that our purposes and expectations are organized around relationships. If relationships become void, the structure of meaning centred upon the relationship disintegrates:

> Nothing becomes meaningful until it can be placed in a context of habits of feeling, principles of conduct, attachments, purposes, conceptions of how people behave: and the attachments which make life meaningful are characteristically specific.

Therefore, the nurturing of our relationships helps us to slowly make meaning of this trauma. "The meaning of change will rarely be clear at the outset" (Fullan, 1991, p. 31).

Still, how do I come to terms with the change?

> No one can resolve the crisis of reintegration on behalf of another. Every attempt to preempt conflict, argument, protest by rational planning, can only be abortive: however reasonable the proposed changes, the process of implementing them must still allow the impulse of rejection to play itself out. When those who have power to manipulate changes act as if they have only to explain, and when their explanations are not at once accepted, shrug off the meaning of lives other than their own. For the reformers have already assimilated these changes to their purposes, and worked out a reformulation that makes sense to them, perhaps through months or years of analysis and debate. If they deny others the chance to do the same, they treat them as puppets dangling by the threads of their own conceptions. (Marris, 1974, p. 155)

I believe that the way we construct the meaning of life and learn to accept change is by interacting with emotions and coming to realize that the experience of attachment is primary and that meaning without attachment is fundamentally inconceivable like the spider without a web. Daily I negotiate and construct meaning with the help of family and friends. Throughout life, our security is built upon attachments. Attachments support our understanding of and our place within the world. As we experience change, these principles that have guided and allowed us to interpret our worlds are bruised. We experience a sense of grief and loss. But as we reflect on the change, we are able to apply meaning and the healing process takes place.

This learning and adaptation, the integrating of thoughts, emotions, and behaviors, this process is taking place within the framework of my doctoral program. And how is this happening? Dr. Shute, my program advisor, has provided me with an anchor and the thread to spin my web.

I think back to my initial interview when I was hoping to gain acceptance into the doctoral program. There was something about the way Dr. Shute asked the questions that confirmed in my mind that I could trust my intuition and respond as myself – that I could be intellectually honest. I avoided the jargon. I remember stating that I only wanted to be accepted in the program if people were willing to support me as a learner.

I remember leaving my interview wondering if I would be accepted, naturally hoping I would. But I also realized that because of my openness about the kind of program I wanted to be involved in, I might have eliminated my chance of acceptance. This had been the first time I had shared my feelings about how I hoped I would be encouraged to learn. It was a risk, and yet I wanted to pose questions, read, and philosophize with fellow educators. Correct answers were really not important but honest expression was. Little did I know that all these resources would become my life support system.

How has Dr. Shute supported my quest? He has supported me as a fellow learner, and has provided me with invitations to learn with him. What are these thoughtful qualities that Dr. Shute emanates? Solway (1989) eloquently articulates:

> Good teachers are "mentors, assured, influential, intensely individual . . . intellectually austere . . . accessible . . . authentic – no tricks, no peacock inflations, no windy rhetoric, no psychological compensations for timidity, suspected failure, or professional bitterness. They flourish in the work, not in the perquisites or the reputation, and upheld a standard of excellence by demanding more of themselves than they did of their students. (p. 33)

Indeed, over the course of the program, Dr. Shute has modelled thoughtfulness. He questions, reads avidly, provokes thought, takes risks, and promotes learning that fills the learner's registry, but he also fosters the commenting on and consideration of what is in the registry. He is an agent unto himself who cannot be forced or manipulated or coerced. He makes meaning and constructs knowledge. He understands that for his students to learn he needs to provide them with invitations. He realizes that the mechanistic or technological frame of reference, where we coerce, force, and compel, seldom works. He is a powerful teacher because he models thoughtfulness. He is a professor who has stopped professing disjointed and fragmented information, one who has started being a "universal man." He has become a learner and has invited us as his students to be a part of this learning.

Gardner (1990) maintains that the principal function of leadership is to release human potential. Dr. Shute continually attempts to promote individual growth. As well, he is concerned with building a community of learners. He appears to share Webb's (1991) description of community as "a collective arrangement of individuals which provides for the mitigation of loneliness, the fostering of self-realization, and the increase of mutually-arrived knowledge" (p. 5). Tinder (1980) refers to Plato and Rousseau to support his view about a sense of community:

> Thus in Plato's ideal city, people would be united according to the demands of their own essence; social unity would not infringe upon, but would be the very condition of, personal wholeness. And when Rousseau discussed the "general will," he was trying to formulate the concept of a social will that would be identical with the innermost will of every member of society. Obeying such a will, the citizen would be simultaneously at one with others and wholly free. Both Plato and Rousseau envisaged societies that would join people as full and authentic human beings, not as parts trimmed and shaped to fit into an external order. (p. 3)

My doctoral cohort group has helped me understand the importance of creating meaning through interaction. Tinder (1980) suggests that the ideal community is the harmony of whole and part. The doctoral program is designed around cooperative and collaborative learning opportunities. In essence, the successful applicants into the program become your extended family of learners. Until the completion of the requirements for comprehensives, you take the majority of your courses together in both small and large group settings. This educational journey is the closest to Tinder's concept of ideal community that I have experienced. Our small group during the year and the larger group in the summer provides a structure that supports and fosters a respect for learning. We continue to grapple with philosophical issues such as: What is truth? Is thoughtfulness a disposition? What is the difference between praise and encouragement? Who imposes standards? Can students learn without extrinsic rewards? What is the role of the private sector? This not only occurred in the classroom environment, but permeated our lives. As we climbed the mountain, ate yogurt, experienced dutch oven cooking, had birthday parties, and attended family suppers, our dialogue was around educational issues and values. We shared our professional and personal knowledge. These discussions continue to shape my understanding of learning and teaching.

For the first time in my life I am learning because I want to learn; not to get a job, not to receive more pay, nor to attain a promotion. My true goal is to grow and attempt to cultivate more of my potential. To quote my husband:

> Sooner or later the serious learner goes through a special, very personal experience that is, unfortunately, unknown to many people. Some call it euphoria. Others say it's a kind of mystical experience that propels you into an elevated state of consciousness. A flash of joy. A sense of timelessness as you learn. The experience is unique to each of us, but when it happens, you break through a barrier that separates you from the casual learner. Forever. And from that point on there is no finish line. You learn for the sake of learning. You begin to be addicted to what learning gives you. (Hehr, 1985, p. 6)

I now understand that feeling. I am a learner. There is no finish line for me. I must never stop trying to excel. I hope as a mother, a wife, a teacher, and a friend to share that enthusiasm, that inspiration, with others as I continue in my quest for meaningful growth in my life. Maybe that is what life is all about. We are on a journey continuing along our path, encountering situations and struggling to understand.

We cannot merely pray to You, O God, to end war;
For we know that You have made the world in a way
That man must find his own path to peace
Within himself and with his neighbor.
We cannot merely pray to You, O God, to end starvation;
For you have already given us the resources
With which to feed the entire world
If we would only use them wisely.
We cannot merely pray to You, O God,
To root out prejudice,
For You have already given us eyes
With which to see the good in all men
If we would only use them rightly.
We cannot merely pray to You, O God, to end despair,
For You have already given us the power
To clear away slums and to give hope
If we would only use our power justly.
We cannot merely pray to You, O God, to end disease,
For you have already given us great minds with which
To search out cures and healing,

If we would only use them constructively.

Therefore we pray to You instead, O God,

For strength, determination, and willpower,

To do instead of just to pray,

To become instead of merely to wish.

(Kushner, 1981)

Kent is now staying in the rehabilitation unit at the Calgary General Hospital. He has started coming home during the day on weekends. Even these visits can be traumatic. Recently, his dad and I attempted to move him in his wheelchair to our basement. With great caution, we made it to the last step. We lost control. Within three seconds, Kent's head hit the step, and he was lying on his back in his chair with his dad on top of him. I am sure all of our hearts stopped beating for a few seconds. Together we needed to decide what to do. It was obvious that the leg support on Kent's chair was broken, Dick's hand was sprained and my leg had a big bruise. But how were we going to ensure that Kent was alright? You see, when you can't feel anything in the majority of your body, you don't know if anything is broken. However, together we checked his entire body looking for bruises or breaks. Kent's senses appeared to tell him he was alright. We again learned the importance of trusting the inner self because when the doctor checked him upon his return that evening to the hospital, Kent's sense was reaffirmed. We are looking forward to continued weekend visits and even, within the next few weeks, that he will spend some nights at home.

Physical rehabilitation is a slow and painful process. After two months of very little use, the muscles in his neck and upper arms need to be stretched and then strengthened. But he continues to make progress in terms of improving his physical abilities.

Mentally and emotionally, he continues to amaze us all. Certainly he has times of despair, depression and anger. However, overall optimism prevails. My sister remarked, after spending time with Kent recently, that he is very self aware.

Self awareness is, for me, a philosophical fly caught in our spider's web of thoughtfulness. Within the social, relational context, we have to be willing to look inside to learn. We have to understand and accept ourselves. We have to know our limitations. But more important, we need to recognize and trust our abilities, our emotions, and our connectedness to others. The joy of learning can then transcend our limitations as we continue to construct our web of understanding in order to maximize our abilities.

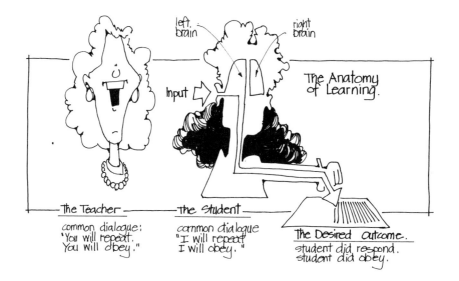

left brain   right brain

Input

The Anatomy of Learning.

The Teacher ——— The Student ———

The Desired Outcome.

common dialogue:
"You will repeat.
You will obey."

common dialogue
"I will repeat"
I will obey."

student did respond.
student did obey.

Altha Neilson was born and raised in Alberta and has a wide background of experience as a teacher and administrator in public schools. She began teaching immediately after high school as a product of the Emergency Teacher Training Program. She completed an undergraduate degree in education at the University of Lethbridge (the slow way, along with the raising of her six children), and a graduate diploma in educational administration and an M.Ed. degree in Teacher Education and Supervision at the University of Calgary. Altha was recently appointed as Superintendent of Schools in the County of Red Deer, and lives on an acreage near Penhold with her husband, Leon.

9

Wasted Times, Wasted Thoughts

Altha Neilson

It was first grade – it was what I had looked forward to for many long months. I had seen my best friend start school a year ahead of me because, although she was about the same age as I was, her birthday was just enough earlier than mine that it was before the cut-off date (she was considered ready for grade one, and I was not). The result was that I had spent the whole year without a playmate, a real one that is. In my loneliness, I had created an imaginary friend, complete with a beautiful name (I thought "Priscilla" was so elegant!), a personality of her own (she was much bolder than I), and a penchant for mischief (I blamed her for everything my mother scolded me for). Priscilla wasn't with me that day however, because it was *my* tears that I was trying to hide by putting my head down in the cubby hole of my table. All the other children sharing that table were busy completing the task that the teacher had assigned to be done; I just couldn't do it. I was devastated! A few minutes before, I had been in line with the other children beside the teacher's desk to have her check my drawing of the three little kittens and their lost mittens. To my dismay, I had apparently misunderstood just what the teacher wanted me to do. I got a big red "X" scrawled on my paper. With flushed face and tears welling up in my eyes, I had hurried to my place and tried to hide my head. What had I done wrong? It certainly wasn't the number concepts involved; I had learned how to count and how to do simple arithmetic long before I went to school. And it wasn't knowledge of the nursery rhymes that was my problem; my mother had been saying them with me for years. Maybe it was my drawing. Or maybe it was that I had not yet learned how to play the school game.

The little blonde girl in the far row of our split grade five/six class was both my idol and my rival. June was a year ahead of me in school; she was in sixth grade and was at the top of the class, so she sat in the row of desks closest to the door. I was just in fifth grade, and my desk was on the other side of the room, but I watched her closely and envied her air of self-assurance that I wished I had. We competed for top marks in math; I must have been working at the same curriculum level as she was, because she definitely considered me a threat. I just wanted to be like her. There was some suggestion by our teacher that I would skip grade six. That would be just perfect! Then maybe I could be part of June's group. However, my hopes were dashed by two events: first, my family decided to move, and I would be going to a new school; but what really told me where I stood and what was important was what June said (so the whole class could hear) when I got a higher mark than she did on the math test that day. I still remember how sharply her words cut: "Oh, you're just the teacher's pet! That's all! You're not really as good in math as I am." Well, maybe I was and maybe I wasn't, but I knew one thing for sure. I was not going to be able to do my best in school and survive. If it was a competition, I didn't like the feeling of being a winner.

By grade nine, I had learned how to play the school game with somewhat more finesse. I could keep my friends if I didn't pay too much attention to my studies and got only acceptably mediocre marks. At this point, since my time was mostly occupied by the opposite sex (at least dreaming about being so occupied), it really didn't take too much effort to stay reasonably lackluster in academic performance. I remember seldom being challenged to do anything more strenuous than memorizing "stuff" (dutifully filling the registry). I got very good at memorizing "stuff," so good in fact that I must have attracted the attention of the high school social studies teacher, who threatened his grade twelve class that a mere grade niner could beat them in a practice run of a departmental examination. I did beat them, but it was no great intellectual accomplishment because most of the exam was made up of multiple-choice questions, and I had learned to play the test game very well by that time. There was little on that exam to perplex or challenge thinking.

What I do recall as a real learning experience during that time of my life was a homework session in which I was trying to understand how a refrigerator works. It was ninth grade science, and we had been given a diagram which I had dutifully colored and labelled, and under which I had neatly copied the notes written on the chalkboard by the teacher. I had copied the notes, but I had no idea of how a refrigerator really worked. The scientific principles involved with expansion and contraction and their relationship to heating and cooling had escaped me. I remember being in the usual process of memorizing my notes in preparation for the regurgitation of them on the test when I found myself actually wanting to know why the refrigerator works as it does. My father was nearby, and although he was not a very patient a teacher, he explained the refrigeration process to me clearly enough so that a light went on in my head, and I felt excited – excited to understand something that had perplexed me, not just to store another piece of "stuff" in the registry. On looking back, I can't recall feeling that excitement about school work very often, and I wonder why not. I did have questions, but I remember wanting only quick and memorizable answers. By that time, I had been well trained in the rules of the school game, the most important of which was to avoid asking real questions, at least, to avoid asking them in school.

The biggest challenge to me in school was in literature class; the challenge was to keep my mouth shut and avoid antagonizing the teacher with anything remotely resembling a contrary point of view. I had learned that the right answers were the answers of the teacher, and that to question those answers, especially those that concerned the making of meaning through the reading of poetry or prose, was simply not smart. Students were not expected to make meaning from what they read if that meaning differed from what the teacher considered to be the correct meaning, the one right answer. In any student-teacher confrontation about interpretations, students usually lost. Occasionally though, just for kicks, a few in the class would suggest some alternative answers. Depending on our persistence and the teacher's patience, the ensuing discussion could make for a bright spot in an otherwise very dreary class. As I remember, there were precious few of those stimulating interludes. High school was mostly just "soak it in and spit it back," which in retrospect was bad enough, but which was made frustratingly worse when, as often was the case, the teacher had obviously only cursory familiarity with the "stuff" and was merely attempting to pour it into the waiting empty heads of students.

This was also the case in French courses throughout my high school study of the subject. No wonder not one member of my class ever learned French well enough even to read aloud from the back of the box of corn flakes! Under the rules of the school game, less-than-effective teachers were just a handicap that students had to live with. At least that handicap offered a challenge of sorts.

By the final year of high school, I was feeling fairly confident in my ability to play the school game well enough to want to help others to learn the rules. I, too, could learn to pour in the "stuff"; I wanted to become a teacher. My first exposure to teacher training was fascinating. I learned all the essentials in six weeks during a summer session at the University of Alberta. At the end of my first instalment of the Emergency Teacher Training Program, I had memorized the parts of the various body systems so that I could teach health, I knew how to balance a school register so that I could satisfy administrative deadlines in a school, and I could chlorinate a well so as to provide safe drinking water for my students (although I never did teach at one of the few rural schools left in Alberta at that time with such primitive amenities). I had been instructed by professors at the university who modelled for us, as student teachers, the ultimate in effective pouring of the "stuff" into our waiting empty heads. They were the masters of the school game.

I remember particularly one final test we had in educational psychology. The exam consisted of only one question: "What have you learned in this class?" I aced that test. My specialty was feeding back the teacher's exact words to answer a question, and I wrote my notes verbatim in their entirety from memory. To this day however, I don't recall one significant thing that I learned in that class. I certainly never had a question about the content; it was all accepted and stored in the registry, but not considered at all. By that time I had spent twelve years and six weeks in formal educational settings, and I had not really learned very much. I had not questioned. I had managed to suppress any perplexity that had surfaced in my mind. Why?

There was one window of insight that I experienced in my initial teacher education program. It came in the form of a course that I don't even recall the title of, but I vividly remember the professor, and what I felt as a result of his teaching. To one who had learned well the rules of the school game, it was strange and uncomfortable for me, at first, to be given rather vague, open-ended instructions as to what was expected for learning in the course. There was choice in what we would study, what we would read, and what we would write about. There was even choice as to how we would demonstrate that we had learned. I found it difficult to make such decisions on my own. I wanted to know what exactly was to be done, and how exactly I was to do it. The professor would only suggest possibilities. It was strange to me, and I didn't handle the ambiguity and the freedom to choose very well.

I also learned a more important lesson from this man, probably one which was a turning point for me. I learned that real teaching involves almost a touching of the spirits, the teacher's and the student's, and it is when that touching of spirits occurs, that learning is indelibly etched in the mind, forever to be a part of the meaning constructed by that mind as it seeks to understand.

The professor was explaining to us something about the need for teachers to accept and work with a student's individuality. He gave examples and reasons and methods, but it was when he described the learning difficulties his own son had experienced that each one of us in the class really listened. I listened, and I understood. He made me *feel,* and I learned.

As I began teaching, I patterned myself at first after the models with which I was the most familiar and the most comfortable. I poured in the "stuff." I told myself that I was doing a good job when my students really spit it back well. Teaching was a snap! Get organized, get their attention, and get on with the routine. I didn't have time for questions, either to answer many for students (typically there weren't many anyway) or to ask many of my own. There simply wasn't time. For the first few years, I was occupied with making neat and tidy lesson plans, very detailed, and checking off each step as it was completed. My students did a lot of checking off too, and filling in the blank spaces, and completing the sentences with the right word (the one *I* was thinking of at the time). Teaching this way was much like learning this way; it was rather boring and somewhat mindless. But I was lucky, I guess, because my students were in the junior high school, and some had reached the stage in learning how to play the school game where they would use the same strategies I had used as a student to provoke a thoughtful interlude, a break in the regularity. They would ask real questions. On the receiving end this time, I found that those interludes became the most exciting and stimulating part of my teaching day. I was engaged for a brief space of time in authentic inquiry with my students about important questions. As I look back, I realize that we became a community of learners, discussing ideas, exchanging thoughts, and sharing in perplexity. However short were the moments that we could spare for such authentic education, I found them to be extremely satisfying and provocative at the same time. I often wished that the students would initiate these sessions more often; I couldn't do that as a teacher. My job was to model the right way to play the school game.

As stimulating as I found my interactions with students in the classroom, the same sort of thing seldom happened within the community of the teaching staff in the schools where I worked. Discussions with colleagues were most often mundane; staffroom talk was limited to topics involving people and things, seldom ideas. How was it possible for a group of such supposedly intelligent people as teachers are purported to be to spend so much time talking about so little? But that was the norm in those schools, and I conformed to the norm. Perhaps the job of teaching school precludes the work of the mind, that considering and pondering of the "stuff" so as to make personal meaning. Perhaps the constant steady rush of interactive events in a teacher's day leaves little time for thought. Perhaps the general mindlessness permeating society today has forced schools to default to the same state. In any case, it wasn't until I began working out of the school district central office in a job which required that I spend considerable time in my car travelling from school to school that I found I had time to think, time for thoughtfulness. I found that as I was driving, when only part of my mental capacity was required in order to get where I was going, I could take the time to do what I now recognize as predicative thinking. I could ponder and consider the things I had put in my registry, and I could attempt to make some meaning out of them in the context of my life at that moment. I could plan about how I would use what I had learned, or consider how the meaning I had made then might alter my future thinking. I could generate other possibilities, other directions, other questions. I had time for thoughtfulness, but I still considered it a luxury which I had to snatch when I could, but which certainly otherwise did not fit in my regular busy schedule. It was almost as if thinking were a frivolous and forbidden pleasure.

It was at this stage on my journey toward thoughtfulness that I began my doctoral studies at Brigham Young University. I was unprepared for the gigantic leap I would be expected to make. The mindset I had to change was not the same as that of my colleagues in the cohort of doctoral students. When Dr. Shute, the program director, told us at our initial meeting in Calgary in the spring of 1990 that he would be introducing us to a new mindset, I believe that what he had in mind was not the change that would be the most profound one for me. I already knew that public schooling, as it exists now, is in deep trouble. I had been a part of the educational system for most of my life either as a student or as a teacher. I had become a master at the school game; I knew that it was mindless. What was a shock to me was that I would now be expected to *think*, and that expectation had never been a part of what I had known to this time.

How did I get this far on my journey, spending such a significant part of my life involved in education, with so few glimpses of thoughtfulness in that system? I am not atypical: I had a fairly normal middle-class upbringing in a relatively typical family situation and attended regular public schools in Alberta. I was not underprivileged or handicapped. I am sure I am not unlike many, many others who have been "educated" in our schools. Why so many wasted times, so many wasted thoughts? Why was I so sure, from the very beginning of my formal education, that it was all-important to learn to play the school game? Perhaps this happened because the school game is the hidden curriculum of the educational system, at least in North America. Gardner (1991) seems to believe this when he explains:

> One of the consequences of the current situation is that many people unjustifiably deemed successes, as well as many needless casualties, emerge from contemporary education systems. Those students who exhibit the canonical (in our terms "scholastic") mind are credited with understanding, even when real understanding is limited or absent. (p. 12)

The school game has winners and losers. I suppose by some criteria, I should consider myself a winner, but I don't. I regret all those times when I could have asked questions, but I didn't, and when I could have been perplexed, but I wasn't. Gardner further elaborates on the rules of the game:

> In schools – including "good" schools – all over the world, we have come to accept certain performances as signals of knowledge or understanding. If you answer questions on a multiple choice test in a certain way, or carry out a problem set in a specified manner, you will be credited with understanding. No one ever asks the further question "But do you *really* understand?" because that would violate an unwritten agreement. (p. 6)

Surely education should be more than this.

Mitchell (1989) describes the primary activity in schools as "induction"- the filling of the registry – as opposed to "education" which involves a leading out. Solway (1989) attributes the problem to the technological world view ("le virage technologique") which has come to dominate education in modern times. We want to believe that teaching and learning can be compared with other enterprises in the industrial and scientific scene. "Efficient," "effective," performance standards," "productivity," and a host of other quantifying terms have been borrowed and applied to education. So far has this trend driven educational policy and practice that in most classrooms, the ideal of thoughtfulness has been replaced with a mindlessness. Thoughtfulness is not efficiency. In the opinion of Glasser (1969), this need to make education more scientific has given rise to a new definition, one that would equate education with memory alone. In his words:

> Education does not emphasize thinking and is so memory-oriented because almost all schools and colleges are dominated by the *certainty principle*. According to the certainty principle, there is a right and a wrong answer to every question; the function of education is then to ensure that each student knows the right answers to a series of questions that educators have decided are important. . . . The unusual child who questions the certainty principle . . . will soon learn that although his thinking may receive brief recognition, in the end, regardless of how thoughtful his discussion may be, the payoff is the right answer. (pp. 3637) *ask about*.

I learned very early about the certainty principle, in first grade, in fact. The three little kittens taught me that lesson. I went on further to learn more rules of the school game such as those listed by Aspy (1986):

> . . . learning consists mostly of memorization . . . thinking and memory relate to pseudo-problems rather than real-life situations . . . in order to teach, teachers must talk most of the time . . . students must listen . . . teaching is telling and learning is listening . . . in order to learn, we sit in straight rows . . . people do not get excited about learning. (p. 57)

Typically there is such a lack of excitement in schools about learning that Fullan (1991) identifies it as the major cause of our educational malaise when he states that "the core problem is that education as it is now practiced does not engage students, teachers, parents, or administrators" (p. 203).

The much-touted and loudly disputed educational reform efforts of the past decade have not worked. Any alterations to schools that have taken place have been mostly "cosmetic and not fundamental" (Sarason, 1990). We have been engaged in making those changes in the packaging of education that may appear to make the product sell better, but there has been no significant general improvement in schooling, and not much lessening of those problems which initiated criticism and the ensuing reform efforts in the first place. Teachers still teach much as they were taught; they pass on to a new generation the rules of the school game. When I was in the classroom, I did this well, so I was judged to be a successful teacher. But I seldom had the time or the incentive to do what Mitchell (1989) would call predicative teaching, the essential follow-up to the accumulation of information in the registry of the mind. That is the process of carefully considering what has gone into the registry with a view to making meaning, seeing connections, developing insights, and perhaps creating new ways of using the information. It is what gives rise to the action, to the new behavior, to the change in the individual which we consider to be learning. It makes the "predicate." Without it, learning becomes merely an exercise in filling memory files with information, useless unless followed by the thoughtful consideration of the files. Without it, our learning is much like a subject without a predicate. Thoughtfulness should be the objective of the whole educational enterprise.

If this is to be, then schools must provide a thoughtful environment for both the adults and the children in the system. Teachers, as well as students, must be "visibly engaged in inquiry, discovery, learning, collaborative problem solving, and critical thinking" (Brown, 1991, p. 233). Barth (1991) makes the observation that the current situation in schools reminds him of the oxygen mask demonstration that is given at the outset of each plane trip he takes, wherein adults are cautioned to place the mask over their own faces first before they go to the assistance of children:

> The fact of the matter is, of course, that the adult must be alive in order to help the child. In schools, we spend a great deal of time placing oxygen masks on other people's faces while we ourselves are suffocating. Principals, preoccupied with expected outcomes, desperately want teachers to breathe in new ideas, yet do not themselves engage in visible, serious learning. Teachers badly want their students to perform at grade level, yet seldom reveal themselves to children as learners. It is small wonder that anyone learns anything in schools. (p. 42)

A school must become a "community of learners, a place where students and adults alike are engaged as active learners in matters of special importance to them and where everyone is thereby encouraging everyone else's learning" (Barth, 1991, p. 9). A school must become a good place to learn for both adults and children. Teachers must not feel compelled, as I did in my classroom, to teach the rules of the school game, nor feel guilty, as I did, about those stolen interludes of authentic education time when students and teachers together pursue perplexity.

Such a new vision for education will not be easy, nor will it be tidy, but it will require one thing for certain, and that is a commitment to the best use of the mind on the part of all the stakeholders. It will require that we engage the thinking of all in an environment conducive to collaborative problem-solving. It will require that we become a community of learners. It will require a disposition of thoughtfulness.

There are some perceptive observers of the educational scene who are becoming skeptical of the possibility of such a change ever coming about, among them Gibboney (1991), who states:

I am concerned about public schooling because this great institution seems unable to renew itself. It seems incapable of marshalling the intelligence and the will necessary to meet the demands that society and our own professional standards have placed upon it. (p. 683)

There are those also who see the formidable task of reforming education as crucial. Sarason (1990) believes that what happens in our schools "is fateful for society" (p. 1), not only in America, but in the world. To Sarason, the fundamental question in educational reform, given the massive problems facing the global community, is: "How can we liberate the human mind to use its capacities in ways that are productively expressive of those capacities at the same time that they strengthen a sense of community?" (p. 1). Others see the challenges presented to humanity at this critical time in history as making the need for thoughtful education crucial to our survival on this planet. Botkin et al (1979) contend that the engagement of people in the enhancement of the use of the human mind is urgent, as they explain:

Humanity is entering a period of extreme alternatives. At the time that an era of scientific and technological advancement has brought us unparalleled knowledge and power, we are witnessing the sudden emergence of a "world problematique" – an enormous tangle of problems in sectors such as energy, population, and food which confront us with unexpected complexity. Unprecedented human fulfillment and ultimate catastrophe are both possible. (p. 1)

The problems facing humanity in the *world problematique* are such that old solutions and old ways of solving problems will not suffice. Humanity lacks the wisdom to untangle the mess; there is a critical need for thoughtfulness.

As I struggle, along with the other doctoral students in our cohort, to make personal meaning of all that we have encountered in the past two years of learning experiences, I wonder what is my role in all this. How can I make a difference? How can I possibly do anything to be a part of the solution for the *world problematique*? And then I remember the professor whose spirit touched mine so many years ago at the beginning of my teacher education, and I get a glimpse of the possibilities. I think of the words of Kapp (1978):

I believe that if the teacher is ever to be allowed into the private, sacred realm of the [student's] heart, where lasting change takes place and lasting imprints are made, a sensitivity to the inner spirit of each [student] and a reverence for teaching moments is required. This sensitivity is difficult to teach, but it is unquestionably the most important quality to be learned. (preface)

I am a teacher. I am once again renewed in my commitment to be a learner and a teacher, to be a sensitive teacher, and to allow no more wasted times or wasted thoughts to steal the opportunities I may have to be a part of humanity's quest for thoughtfulness.

Ron Patrick was born and raised in Dawson Creek, British Columbia, the eldest of three children. Following high school, Ron served a two year mission in Kentucky and Tennessee. He obtained B.Ed. and M.Ed. degrees at the University of Alberta in Edmonton, where he currently works for the Church Education System as an instructor at the Institute of Religion adjacent to the university campus. Ron has been a public school elementary and junior high school teacher and principal. He loves the outdoors and canoeing, hiking, fishing, and skiing in the mountains. Ron and his wife, Arja, who is also a teacher, have five sons and one daughter.

10

Thinking About Truth

Ron Patrick

I know everything. I first knew everything when I was two years old, but I have been reluctant to tell many people. You see, the idea has never gone over very well.

I specifically recall as a five-year-old sandbox owner that my mother told me to play nicely with the neighborhood children. Since I already knew that, I ignored her because I was more interested in maintaining control over my property. Apparently, some of the neighborhood kids had objected to me beating them over the head with a big stick when they refused to understand about me knowing everything. It was more than my perspective; it was my sandbox. Mother gave them permission to return the favor to teach me a lesson. I learned my lesson. I learned that I could know whatever I wanted, as long as I didn't bang people over the head with it. Several similar experiences have taught me to be sensitive about sharing my knowledge with others.

The only other time I have tried to share the notion that "I know everything" was during my teenage years, but no one took me seriously. I suspect that bringing it up again during mid-life crisis isn't going to make much of an impact either.

I don't really see what the problem is. Others get to know everything. Take my wife's family, for example. You can hardly shut them up for everything that they know. It would amaze you what they know about how we spend our money and raise our children. Speaking of children – mine know everything. Most kids do. Think about it; who do you personally know that doesn't know everything? Sure, the idiot that cuts you off in traffic or holds up the line in MacDonald's doesn't know much, but real people know everything. Have you ever paid attention to the people that write newspapers, teach school, run industry, operate banks, loan books, sell cars, follow sports, teach religion, administer universities, hold public office, or manage parking lots? Even bank machines, computers, and telephone answering systems know everything! Since everybody knows so much, why don't we have all the answers? For a planet that is celebrating so much advanced technology and accumulated knowledge, why are there more questions than answers?

Man's reason stretches from the ability to observe exactly eight subatomic neutrinos trapped 2 000 feet beneath Lake Erie in a pitch dark tank, to their source beyond the Milky Way in the Tarantula Nebula, the Sanduleak Supernova, a hot blue star with 20 times the sun's mass which exploded a relatively close 170 000 light years away. If all the people that knew so much would think about the astonishing and marvelous knowledge that we possess, would we be so reluctant to share what we know?

At Princeton University, researchers are refitting a doughnut-shaped machine called a "tokamak" in an attempt to achieve the elusive break-even point at which energy released by fusion equals that required to produce it. Using powerful magnets to confine a superhot ring of gas, the tokamak heats the nuclei of hydrogen isotopes extracted from water until they fuse together, releasing energy. The method has not yet demonstrated that a self-sustaining fusion reaction is practical. However if they ever do, our worries about electricity will be over.

Virtual reality, a new application of supercomputers, feeds stimuli directly into the brain through vision and hearing, which simulates any environment that the operator wishes to create in his or her imagination. The advanced equipment will be completely interactive so that the mind will experience virtual reality, indistinguishable from what is real. Applications of VR will permit doctors to travel inside the body of their patients and assist architects to modify specifications after their clients have toured their new home.

See, I told you that I knew everything – well almost. One of the things I do know is that you and I are living at one of the most exciting, exhilarating, and wonderful times in the history of the planet earth. Man has never known more or had greater opportunities to learn. Homo sapiens have infinite potential for growth, leadership, and the release of human possibilities. We as individuals, nations, and people face an awesome future. I know that the most golden of all golden ages is before us, and I am glad I have written this down, because when the day arrives, I will remember, and show you this page.

Unfortunately, while many current events have given much hope and promise, there is much trouble, strife, and terror in the world. We are concerned about the fall of Communism and the ability of newly established democratic governments to change and adapt economic systems throughout the world quickly enough to avoid deprivation and hardship. The world suffers from economic disparity, political unrest, environmental devastation, disease, crime, natural disasters, and death. However, the problems and the questions are the fuel that will bring the golden age.

This, my personal journey, is supposed to be about thinking, learning, teaching and being thoughtful. I have had a difficult time with the assignment because I have been trying too hard to think about something thoughtful. I spent so much time thinking about thinking that I didn't know what to think. So I gave up the idea and decided to think about some things that are really important to me. When I thought about the world and skimmed through a stack of National Geographic magazines, I couldn't help but think about all the people in the world who are struggling – struggling to live, struggling to love and be loved, and struggling to find meaning in a world that is often cruel and difficult.

As I was thinking about the misfortunes and tragedies in the lives of others, I became overwhelmed at my good fortune in living in a promised land flowing with abundance, in the company of great people who live happy, healthy, productive lives. I am so grateful for a wonderful family and a terrific educational experience which prepared me for a career in teaching that has been exciting, fulfilling, and rewarding. I have been troubled to learn that many have had negative experiences in schools, and I hope that my thoughts will assist others in understanding that learning and teaching can and should be an interesting and positive experience for everyone in schools. Permit me to pay tribute to my parents, teachers, friends, and colleagues through a brief synopsis of my personal educational journey.

I thank the wonderful teachers and friends that cared for me as I attended my thirteen years of public school in Dawson Creek, British Columbia. They taught me to read, talk, laugh, play, learn, and appreciate the wonders of the natural world we live in. (My wife wishes that they had taught me how to dance.) They gave me love, courage, responsibility, and confidence. I came away with sweet memories of happy days, good friends, and moral role models.

The second best part about going to university to get a teaching degree when you are married and starting a family which complains about how poor you are. The best part is that all your friends are in the same boat. Our "tough" times while at university were some of our happiest times.

I have spent most of my teaching career with teenagers in the middle schools and have loved every minute of it. My philosophy of teaching has been that a little bit of sugar helps the medicine go down, and I have really tried to not take the whole thing too seriously. The four schools I have worked in had excellent students and great teachers with supportive parents, school board trustees, and central office personnel. Even though I left the public school four years ago to work in church education, I still get a little misty thinking about the good days we had.

For the balance of the story of my journey, I would like to address some of the questions which have caused me great perplexity, and if I don't come up with any answers, at least I will have asked the questions. In the interest of time and space, I have abandoned trying to summarize all I know, which, if you remember, is a lot. My purpose will be to consider some of the issues of educational leadership which seem important to me.

I began by being "silly" about knowing everything. What I think is really silly is that we know far more than we are willing or able to act upon. We know many things we could do about our schools which could bring about positive results, but because of political or financial reasons, we sacrifice our educational responsibilities. For example, many schools fail to inform the public about their educational merit and lose credibility with the large population of taxpayers who no longer have children in school. Educators know public relations are important, but somehow we forget, and say that we are too busy. We also know that change in schools comes from within and must take teachers and principals into account. Why are local or provincial jurisdictions not supporting cooperative levels of curriculum development or educational change in schools? Why are schools often reluctant to involve teachers in educational decision-making?

The preceding examples are only symptoms of the real problem hindering educational leadership. The real problem is the technological and mechanistic frame of reference that currently drives the world in which we live and all the systems that derive from it, including the educational system. Discussion of the technological world view has been a dominant theme throughout this book. I wish to examine it from a philosophical point of view, to emphasize that it is not technology that is so damaging, but humanism, which places man at the centre of the universe.

Bloom (1987) reveals the danger of humanism in the opening pages of his book, *The Closing of the American Mind.* He begins by saying "almost every student entering the university believes, or says he believes, that truth is relative" (p. 25). If truth is relative, every one is free to do his own thing, because there are no clear moral standards. Bloom explains that the way students see this idea is that "the relativity of truth is not a theoretical insight but a moral postulate, the condition of a free society . . . " (p. 25). He observes that "relativism is necessary to openness, and this is the virtue, the only virtue, which all primary education for more than fifty years has dedicated itself to inculcating" (p. 26).

Bloom challenges this "great insight of our times" and facetiously warns that the "true believer is the real danger." He summarizes the issue in these words: "The point is not to correct the mistakes and really be right; rather it is not to think you are right at all" (p. 26). Bloom's identification of the problem is cautious, because he realizes how pervasive the tenets of humanism are. His book carefully demonstrates the ramifications of how insidious this threat is to the closing of the American mind. When Bloom first wrote the book, he had no idea that his unveiling of the problem would cause such a stir. Following publication, Bloom's book became an immediate best-seller. Reviewers called the book, "chilling," "radical," "electric-shock therapy," "sweetly reasoned and outraged," and "passionate and witty." Bloom was described as a thinker who was willing to take risks. It is an understatement that Bloom hit the "nerve" of the prevailing Western world view, and the reaction was anything but positive. Nearly every aspect of his argument and validations was actively challenged and attacked in the media and the press (Stone,1989). Bloom's exposure of relativism and the reaction of the critics is persuasive evidence of the prevailing world view that the Russian scholar, Solzhenitsyn (1978), describes as the "calamity of an autonomous, irreligious humanistic consciousness . . . it has made man the measure of all things on earth – imperfect man, who is never free of pride, self-interest, envy, vanity, and dozens of other defects" (p. 2). Solzhenitsyn gives a marvelous description of how this predominant frame of reference can affect the motives and actions of people who wittingly or unwittingly buy in to such a perspective. Good is whatever brings pleasure and bad is whatever hurts people. This anthropocentric world view promotes indiscriminate freedom in the name of the democratic social contract.

The crux of the matter is that society decries those that claim "knowledge," yet is disposed to grant you whatever "beliefs" you dare to offer. Within such a society, we politely and politically fawn one another's beliefs, while inwardly noting that everyone is entitled to his own perspective. We lack integrity and moral honesty. Furthermore, when we talk about "creating" or "constructing" personal knowledge, we dumbly buy in by building our own rules of conduct. While personal meaning allows us the individual freedom to create an acceptable world of our own, it can isolate us from the real world that we might truly hope to understand. In practice, we may listen to what people have to say, but we never really hear what they are saying because life becomes a game.

I realize that anthropocentrism is probably preferable to a theocratic-type regime because we have the freedom to know whatever we want, but it makes the discovery of "real" truth so lonesome because everyone thinks that we are "just doing our own thing." My thesis is that we must foster and encourage the search for truth – the real truth, the whole truth. Remember in the beginning when I said I was being silly about knowing everything; that was just to capture attention. I was absolutely serious about knowing some things that are "really" true. But the truth is not easily given away; every person has to find it on his or her own. I just get impatient when it seems so obvious to me, because we get "blinded by the light."

This is the reason why it is so important to develop an interrogative mind, to constantly question, seek, ask, ponder, and reflect on what is happening around us. There are thousands of examples in the lives of people when the truth was staring them in the face, but they could not see it. Langer (1989), in her book, *Mindfulness,* gives some wonderful examples. Allow me to share one of my personal examples. I was certain that my wife was losing her hearing, so

I decided to test her by calling her name from another room. After three attempts, each increasingly louder, I finally triumphantly went to her to confront her with my research. As I faced her, she looked at me with a puzzled expression, and said, "What did you want? I answered three times. Didn't you hear me?" Foiled again, I asked, "Do you want to dance?"

During the first summer at BYU, we were given a computer-generated dot picture which, when placed at the correct focal point from the eyes, suddenly reveals a three- dimensional image which reads, "Seeing the light." When you are in focus and can see the hidden image, it is great, but when you are out of focus or can't see it, you either get angry or throw it away. This "truth" business is similar. We often discard something too quickly or go beyond the mark. Truth distills upon our senses and is revealed in moments of serenity, after we have pondered what we have learned. The interrogative mind provides knowledge, but meditation and thought yield truth.

I believe that when we disagree with someone, it is an invitation to learn. Most of the time when we think someone is off on a frolic, it's because we don't agree with him. That's okay, as long as we are willing to give one another's ideas a chance. There is an interesting phenomenon in Southern Alberta basketball that might illustrate the point. When the referee makes a call, you decide if it's a good or a poor call depending on how it affects your team. I have watched fans argue with the full force of their lungs that their son didn't commit the foul. That's not the way to look for truth. That's playing the game, and maybe, if you haven't acted too stupidly, the ref might give your boy a break the next time. However, the "real" truth is that he probably committed the foul. The silly thing is that we get so used to playing the game, we give up looking for the truth because (let's face it) sometimes the truth hurts.

Is it politeness or lack of integrity when we are open to consider someone's knowledge and then dump it as a differing perspective without accepting the challenge to find the truth? Certainly, there are inappropriate or inauspicious times to go for the truth. When my wife asks me if I have had a good time at the dance, she knows not to press the issue. Similarly, if you ever have the chance to taste my "slumgullian" casserole, and I ask you how you like it, I would be wise to ask only once. However, if you really want to know something, you have to be persistent.

Throughout the BYU program, we have been fond of mountains because, I suppose, there are plenty of lively metaphors we can apply to them. I like mountains because the virtue of the climb takes you out of the world to a place of solitude where you can ponder, reflect, and get a better view of things. It is the place where prophets, stoics, philosophers and boy scouts go. Truth sits on mountains. You may climb the mountain any way you wish. There are popular routes, but climb you must. Others can help you climb the mountain or show you the way, but no one gets carried up the mountain; that's one of the rules. As you travel up the mountain, your vision improves until you reach the summit and the panorama fills your view. The journey up the mountain may differ, but the view at the top is always the same. If we have been in the valley too long and forget the view, we can always return, because the view at the top will still be there. Mountains never change.

Now it is time for a quiz. Frank Smith (1990) is a terrific author who writes very well about thinking and learning. I enjoy his books because what he says seems to make sense. I accept his idea that thinking and learning, like breathing, are natural and necessary functions of living people. For the quiz, consider the following quotation by Frank Smith and tell me what you think. Smith said, "Next to persuading people to change their mind, the hardest thing to do is to persuade them that not everyone sees the world the way they do, or that those who have a different point of view are not necessarily wrong" (p. 29). Does this quote reveal that Smith believes in relativism? If not, how could opposing points of view both be correct? They both could be wrong, but how could they both be right? Perhaps Smith makes an important point, and I should be persuaded to understand that not everyone sees the world the way I do. My experience with women's issues has been a dramatic revelation that I need to be more aware and open to differing points of view. Tolerance and understanding are absolutely essential in the journey to truth.

This kind of discussion reminds me of the Hobbit's reaction to adventures. Bilbo Baggins says: "We are plain quiet folk and I have no use for adventures. Nasty disturbing uncomfortable things! Make you late for dinner! I can't think what anybody sees in them. . . . We don't want any adventures here, thank you!" (Tolkien, 1937, p. 16) Often the struggle to sort out our own biases and recognize our own prejudices can be nasty and uncomfortable. At the start, when I said I knew everything, please understand that it has no relevance to this present discussion. No one can ever know what another person feels or has experienced even if he walks a mile in the other person's shoes. Each personal journey carries its own secrets and burdens. If I have been bold in my writing, my intention is not to offend or upset. If I have done so, I am very sorry. I offer my deepest respect to the family of man. Thoughtfulness includes the idea that we need to be thoughtful of one another, and I am trying to improve that quality in my relationships.

The next important issue I would like to write about is how to describe the theocentric world view as an alternative that is much more successful when it is introduced by persuasion rather than by force. Bloom (1978) says that in order to make humanism work, "there was a conscious, if covert, effort to weaken religious beliefs . . . to the realm of opinion as opposed to knowledge"

(p. 28). I would like to put some effort into persuading you that voluntary theocentrism is neither oppressive nor scary.

Solzhenitsyn (1978) explains that when Western civilization "lost the concept of a Supreme Complete Entity which used to restrain our passions and our irresponsibility," we placed our faith in mankind's politics and social reforms, "only to find out that we were being deprived of our most precious possession: our spiritual life" (p. 57). Spiritual life recognizes the existence of a Divine Creator. Since we live in a lone and dreary world subject to death, pain, and sorrow, the theocentric alternative teaches that there is purpose to life. The purpose of life is revealed to man by God. Solzhenitsyn argues that since man is doomed to death, "his task on earth evidently must be more spiritual . . . it has to be the fulfillment of a permanent, earnest duty so that one's life journey may become above all an experience of moral growth: to leave life a better human being than one started it" (p. 59). Unfortunately, one of the most popular and legitimate criticisms of religious thought is that we talk a better story than we act. There is no excuse for that. We all would rather see a sermon than hear one any day. My explanation of this problem is that most religionists haven't really thought about what they believe. They practice religion from a humanistic point of view. They believe what they want to believe just because it feels good. Man-made religion is anthropocentrism in sheep's clothing. Only true religion undefiled can teach principles of truth, and that is why real prophets pay a higher price.

My interest in describing the theocentric alternative is that it is the only source of essential knowledge that can provide strong enough convictions to guide man's action. Stephen Hawking has earned an international reputation as the most brilliant theoretical physicist since Einstein. According to Hawking (1988), "Any physical theory is always provisional, in the sense that it is only a hypothesis: you can never prove it" (p. 10). Truth can always be proven. The reason the anthropocentric learner is always learning and never coming to a knowledge of the truth is that his truth is relative – it keeps changing. Hawking understands this limitation of man's reason and indicates the ultimate source of truth. Hawking states:

> Today we still yearn to know why we are here and where we came from. Humanity's deepest desire for knowledge is justification enough for our continuing quest. . . . Up to now, most scientists have been too occupied with the development of new theories that describe what the universe is to ask the question why . . . the discussion of the question of why it is that we and the universe exist. If we find the answer to that, it would be the ultimate triumph of human reason – for then we would know the mind of God. (p. 175)

Education must be more than what Ortega y Gasset (1944) describes as mere "ornamentation." Education must fascinate and inspire the soul. Learning and thinking is a natural disposition of the mind. "Think, man, think." The real world should not be cut up, atomized, or categorized into the man-made divisions of religion, politics, society or culture. Everything is real. We need to look for truth wherever we can find it. Page Smith (1990) in concluding his book, *Killing The Spirit*, quotes Whitehead (1929) as follows: "The essence of education . . . is that it be religious" (p. 297). This does not mean that we teach religion in schools. It means we think, ponder, and seek for truth. Whitehead's idea that education be religious means that it be real and authentic.

Our resistance to the idea that there is absolute truth is that we suppose that schools must become dogmatic dispensers of right answers. Wrong. A true theocentric voluntary frame of reference demands that we question, ask, and prove all things. Smith (1990) argues that the way to improve thinking in schools is that "students – and teachers – must learn to doubt" (p. 129). Smith is correct; perplexity is the key to learning. He says:

> Certainty stunts thought, in ourselves and others. The fruits of understanding grow from seeds of doubt. All thinking is based on "suppose things were different." Critical thinking begins with readiness to challenge received wisdom. Creative thinking is the opposite of logic; it considers all alternatives and resists mechanistic modes of decision making. Thought flourishes as questions are asked, not as answers are found. (p. 129)

Smith advises students and teachers to learn to withhold judgment, challenge, and be challenged by others.

Please do not misunderstand. The invitation to find truth is not to give you the ultimate answer. All I ask is that you withhold judgment, interrogate, think and ponder, and allow your mind and spirit to consider all the alternatives.

According to Barzun (1991):

> Schools are not intended to moralize a wicked world but to impart knowledge and develop intelligence, with only two social aims in mind: prepare to take one's share in the world's work and perhaps in addition, lend a hand in improving society, after schooling is done. . . . All that . . . Good-Samaritan courses amount to is pieties. They present moralizing mixed with anecdotes . . . the best and worst students alike are bored. . . nor do they relish continual preachiness any better than adults. (p. 50)

Servant leadership is the best way to teach truth. Christ taught that "he that is greatest among you shall be your servant" (Matthew 22:10). The best service we can provide to one another is unconditional love and respect. Much has been written about the importance of the heart. I would say that the spirit is important too. Teaching requires the heart, mind, and soul.

Fromm (1976) explains that if we deceive ourselves, we become subject to the social world around us. He states:

... knowing begins with the awareness of the deceptiveness of our common sense perceptions, in the sense that our picture of physical reality does not correspond to what is "really real" ... what we hold to be true and self-evident is illusion produced by the suggestive influence of the social world in which we live. (p. 29)

I hope that we will not do that, but will seek for knowledge and be blessed with truth.

Even though we are strongly influenced by a "zeitgeist" which is difficult if not impossible to shrug off, let us foster questions, seeking, learning, teaching, and thinking. In our educational leadership experience, we have learned the importance of providing models for student learning. Page Smith (1990) states:

The point I wish to make is a simple one. There is no decent, adequate, respectable education, in the proper sense of that much-abused word, without personal involvement by a teacher with the needs and concerns, academic and personal, of his/her students. (p. 7).

In conclusion, I wish to thank my teacher for his great caring and example, and my colleagues, who have been most patient with a person who always acts as if he knows everything and keeps hitting them over the head. You have taught me so much – thank you for your service. I hope you will let me be your servant.

References

Alberta Education. (1989). *Teaching thinking.* Edmonton, Alberta.

Alberta Education. (1991). *Vision for the nineties . . . a plan of action.* Edmonton, Alberta.

Aspy, D. M. (1986). *This is school! Sit down and listen!* Amherst, MA: Human Resources Development Press.

Barell, J. (1991). *Teaching for thoughtfulness.* New York: Longman.

Barth, R. (1991). *Improving schools from within.* San Francisco: Jossey-Bass.

Barzun, J. (1991). *Begin here: The forgotten conditions of teaching and learning.* Chicago: University of Chicago Press.

Bennis, W. (1990). *Why leaders can't lead.* San Francisco: Jossey-Bass.

Bennis, W. & Nanus, B. (1985). *Leaders, the strategies for taking charge.* New York: Harper & Row.

Block, P. (1987). *The empowered manager.* San Francisco: Jossey-Bass.

Bloom, A. *The closing of the American mind.* New York: Simon & Schuster.

Bollnow, O. F. (1989). The pedagogical atmosphere: The perspective of the child. *Phenomenology and Pedagogy, 7,*

Botkin, J. et al. (1979). *No limits to learning.* Oxford: Pergammon Press.

Brigham Young University. (1989). *Doctor of education program announcement.* Provo, UT.

Brown, R. (1985, April). Barriers to thoughtfulness. *Basic Education,* pp. 4-7.

Brown, R. (1987). Who is accountable for thoughtfulness? *Phi Delta_Kappan,* 69(1), 49-52.

Brown, R. (1988, Spring). Schooling and thoughtfulness. *Basic Education: Issues, Answers & Facts, 3*(3), 2-6.

Brown, R. (1988, May). An agenda for thoughtfulness. *Basic Education,* pp. 9-12.

Brown, R. (1989). Testing and thoughtfulness. *Educational Leadership, 46*(7), 31-33.

Brown, R. (1991). *Schools of thought.* San Francisco: Jossey-Bass.

Bruner, J. (1990). *Acts of meaning.* Cambridge: Harvard University Press.

Capra, F. (1988). *The turning point.* Toronto: Bantam Books.

City man is shot. (1991,October). *Calgary Herald,* p. 1.

The coalition of essential schools. *Horace, 6*(3)

Cory, W. (1988, Fall). Notes and quotes. *College boards academic connections,* p. 10.

County of Wheatland. (1991, January). *Parent think tank session,* Strathmore, Alberta.

Covey, S. R. (1989). *The 7 habits of highly effective people.* New York: Simon & Schuster.

Desjardin, C. & Osman Brown, C. (1991, January). A new look at leadership styles. *National Forum,*

DePree, M. (1989). *Leadership is an art.* New York: Bantam Doubleday.

Dickens, C. (1961). *Hard times.* Markham, Ontario: Penguin Books.

Dillon, J. T. (1983). *Teaching and the art of questioning.* Bloomington, IN: Phi Delta Kappa.

Dillon, J. T. (1988). *Questioning and teaching: A manual of practice.* New York: Teachers College Press.

Elam, S. M., Rose, L. C. & Gallup, A. M. (1991). The 23rd annual Gallup poll of public attitudes toward public schools. *Phi Delta Kappan, 73*(1), 41-56.

Eisner, E. W. (1981) The role of arts in cognition and curriculum. *Phi Delta Kappan, 63*(1), 48-52.

Flinders, N. (1990, August). *The intellectual faultline in western culture.* Lecture to Brigham Young University doctoral student group, Provo, UT.

Freud, S. (1937). Analysis terminable and interminable. In J. Strachey (Ed.), *The standard edition of the complete works of Sigmund Freud: Vol. XXIII* (1937-39). London: Hogarth Press.

Fromm, E. (1976). *To have or to be.* New York: Harper & Row.

Fullan, M. (1991). *The new meaning of educational change.* New York: Teachers College Press.

Gardner, H. (1991). *The unschooled mind.* New York: Basic Books.

Gardner, J. (1990). *On leadership.* New York: The Free Press.

Gibboney, R. (1991). The killing field of reform. *Phi Delta Kappan, 72*(9), 682-688.

Glasser, W. (1969). *Schools without failure.* New York: Harper & Row.

Goodlad, J. I. (1984). *A place called school.* New York: McGraw Hill.

Graves, D. H. (1990). *The reading/writing teacher's companion. Discover your own literacy.* Portsmouth, NH: Heinemann.

Greene, M. (1985). Consciousness of the public space: Discovering a pedagogy. *Phenomenology and Pedagogy, 3*(2), 69-83.

Greenleaf, R. K. (1977). *Servant Leadership.* New York: Paulist Press.

Hawking, S. (1988). *A brief history of time.* New York: Bantam Books.

Hehr, D. (1985, February). *Teaching-learning: There is no finish line.* Paper presented at Calgary City Teachers' Convention, Calgary, Alberta.

Hirsch, E. D. (1987). *Cultural literacy.* Boston: Houghton Mifflin.

Hooke, R. (1665). *Micrographia.* British Museum.

Katz, L. G. & Chard, S. C. (1991). *Engaging children's minds: The project approach.* New Jersey: Ablex Publishing.

Kapp, A. G. (1978). *The gentle touch.* Salt Lake City: Deseret Books.

Kegan, R. (1982). *The evolving self.* Cambridge: Harvard University Press.

Kushner, H. S. (1981). *When bad things happen to good people.* New York: Avon Books.

Langer, E. J. (1989). *Mindfulness.* New York: Addison Wesley.

Lewis, C. D. (1951). *The poet's task.* London: Oxford University Press.

Man seriously hurt in traffic shooting. (1991, October). *Calgary Sun,* p. 1.

Marris, P. (1975). *Loss and change.* New York: Anchor Press/Doubleday.

Mathews, J. (1988). *Escalante: The best teacher in America.* New York: Henry Holt & Co.

Maddox, S. (1990). *Spinal network.* Colorado: McCormick Design.

McKinnon, G. (1989). *Promoting thoughtfulness in Alberta schools – a study of two principals.* Unpublished manuscript.

McKinnon, G. (1991). *Predicative teaching and learning – a study of teachers and students.* Unpublished manuscript.

Mikulecky, L. (1978). *Aliteracy and a changing view of reading goals.* Paper presented at the 23rd annual meeting of the International Reading Association, Houston, TX.

Mitchell, R. (1981). *The graves of academe.* Toronto: Little, Brown & Co.

Mitchell, R. (1985). Why good grammar? *National Forum, 65*(4), 4-6, 10.

Neatby, H. (1953). *So little for the mind.* Toronto: Clark Irwin.

The new lexicon Webster's encyclopedic dictionary of the English language. (1988). New York: Lexicon Publications.

Ortega y Gasset, J. (1959). *Man and crisis.* London: George Allen & Unwin.

Polanyi, M. (1962). *Personal knowledge.* Chicago: University of Chicago Press.

Raths, L. E. (1986). *Teaching for thinking.* New York: Teachers College Press.

Resnick, L. B. (1987). *Education and learning to think.* Washington, DC: National Academy Press.

Rifkin, J. (1989). *Entropy: Into the greenhouse world.* New York: Bantam.

Sarason, S. (1991). *The predictable failure of educational reform.* San Francisco: Jossey-Bass.

Sacalis, N. (1991, August). Lecture to Brigham Young University doctoral student group, Provo, UT.

Schön, D. (1971). *Beyond the stable state.* New York: Norton.

Schön, D. (1983). *Educating the reflective practitioner.* New York: Basic Books.

Schön, D. (1983). *The reflective practitioner: How professionals think in action.* New York: Basic Books.

Shute, R. W. (1990, July). Lecture to Brigham Young University doctoral student group, Provo, UT.

Shute, R. W. (1991, July). *The Judy paper.* Paper presented to Brigham Young University doctoral student group, Provo, UT.

Sizer, T. R. (1984). *Horace's compromise: The dilemma of the American high school.* Boston: Houghton Mifflin.

Smith, F. (1986). *Insult to intelligence.* New York: Arbor House.

Smith, F. (1988). *Joining the literacy club.* Portsmouth, NH: Heinemann.

Smith, F. (1990). *To think.* New York: Teachers College Press.

Smith, P. (1990). *Killing the spirit.* New York: Viking Penguin.

Solway, D. (1989). *Education lost: Reflections on contemporary pedagogical practice.* Toronto: Ontario Institute for Studies in Education.

Solzhenitsyn, A. (1978, June). *A world split apart.* Commencement address at Harvard University, Cambridge, MA.

Stewart, D. & Mickunis, A. (1974). *Exploring phenomenology.* American Library Association.

Stone, R. L. (1989). *Essays on the closing of the American mind.* Chicago: Chicago Review Press.

Tinder, G. (1980). *Community: Reflections on a tragic ideal.* Shreveport: Louisiana State University Press.

Tolkien, J. R. (1937). *The hobbit.* London: Unwin Hyman.

Tomlinson, T. M. & Cross, C. T. (1991). Student effort: The key to higher standards. *Educational Leadership, 49*(1), 69-73.

Van Manen, M. (1986). *The tone of teaching.* Richmond Hill: Scholastic.

Velikovsky, I. (1950). *Worlds in collision.* London: Gollancz.

Vygotsky, L. (1986). *Thought and language.* Cambridge: Massachusetts Institute of Technology.

Webb, C. D. & Shute, R. W. (1987). Strategies to promote meaningful learning in the college classroom. *Intellectual Skills Development Journal, 3,*(1),

Webb, C. D. (1991, April). *Notes on thoughtful teaching and learning.* Paper presented to Brigham Young University doctoral student group, Calgary, Alberta.

Webb, C. D. (1991, August). *What I learned (or had reinforced by) the conference on thoughtful education.* Lecture to Brigham Young University doctoral student group, Provo, UT.

Webb, C. D. & Shute, R. W. (1989, Winter). Docemur docendo: In teaching we are taught. *The Journal of Professional Studies,* pp. 27-34.

Whitehead, A. N. (1929). *The aims of education and other essays.* New York: Free Press.

Wiggins, (1987, Winter). Creating a thought-provoking curriculum. *American Educator.*

Wiggins, G. (1989). Teaching to the (authentic) test. *Educational Leadership, 46*(7), 41-47.

Wiggins, G. (1989). The futility of trying to teach everything of importance. *Educational Leadership, 42*(3), 44-59.

Wilber, K. (1990). *Eye to eye.* Boston: Shambhala Publications.

Wolf, D. P. (1989). Portfolio assessment: Sampling student work. *Educational Leadership, 46T*(7), 35-39.